MOUNTAIN WALKS
KINDER SCOUT

MOUNTAIN WALKS
KINDER SCOUT

15 ROUTES TO ENJOY ON AND AROUND KINDER

First published in 2024 by Vertebrate Publishing.

Vertebrate Publishing
Omega Court, 352 Cemetery Road, Sheffield S11 8FT, United Kingdom.
www.adventurebooks.com

A CIP catalogue record for this book is available from the British Library.

ISBN 978-1-83981-204-0 (Paperback)
ISBN 978-1-83981-205-7 (Ebook)

Front cover: Looking across to Grindslow Knoll from the head of Grinds Brook.
Back cover: Frosty morning on Kinder Scout.
Photography by Sarah Lister unless otherwise credited.

All maps reproduced by permission of Ordnance Survey
on behalf of The Controller of His Majesty's Stationery Office.
© Crown Copyright. AC0000809882

Map data

Design and production by Jane Beagley
www.adventurebooks.com

Printed and bound in Europe by Latitude Press.

Vertebrate Publishing is committed to printing on paper from sustainable sources.

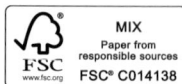

MIX
Paper from
responsible sources
FSC® C014138
FSC
www.fsc.org

MOUNTAIN WALKS
KINDER SCOUT

15 ROUTES TO ENJOY ON AND AROUND KINDER

SARAH LISTER

VP

Vertebrate Publishing, Sheffield
www.adventurebooks.com

Greenfield

Moor

Dovestone Reservoir

Chew Reservoir

468

582

Black Hill

Crow Edge

Edge

Thurlstone

Carlecotes

Winscar Reservoir

Dunford Bridge

Langsett

A628

Salter's Brook Bridge

Windleden Reservoir

Langsett Resr

Upper Midhope

MIDHOPE MOORS

Midh

ST

MOSSLEY

Buckton Vale

Millbrook

BRIDGE

541

523

14

A628

Walkerwood Reservoir

Tintwistle

B6105

Torside Reservoir

River Derwent

HOWDEN MOORS

Hollingworth

m in dale

Longdendale

Pennine Way

633

Bleaklow Hill

546

538

Howden Reservoir

Abbey Brook

Dale Dike Reservoir

Hadfield

adbottom

A6016

Gamesley

GLOSSOP

DOCTOR'S GATE

Snake Pass

Upper Derwent Reservoirs

Strines Reservoir

A626

Charlesworth

Chisworth

stall

Chunal

A57

Featherbed Top

544

ROMAN

River Ashop

Ladybower Reservoir

318

PLE

A624

Kinder Reservoir

14

14

15

13

Little Hayfield

Mellor

327

H

6

Kinder Scout

9

12

H

5

8

590

P

E

A

K

NEW MILLS

A6015

Birch Vale

Hayfield

Edale Cross

Edale

1

3

11

Low Leighton

Furness Vale

452

Chinley Head

10

Pennine Way

4

2

Barber Booth

7

River Noe

Hotel

463

Aston

A6013

Bamford

Newtown

408

Black Hill

Chinley

Tumuli

Hope

Thornhill

Brough

Bradwell

Whaley Bridge

B5470

Slackhall

Sparrowpit

470

Peveril Castle

Castleton

417

Taxal

Chapel-en-le-Frith

A623

Peak Forest

Coplow Dale

Little Hucklow

Abney

Great Hucklow

Stone Circle

Grindle

Fernilee

Dove Holes

Combs Reservoir

507

Combs

A6

Peak Dale

PEAK DISTRICT NATIONAL PARK

Grindlow

Eyam

Eya Ha

Shining Tor 559

Errwood Reservoir

A5004

Upper End

406

Wheston

Tideswell

17

Litton

Foolow

Stoney Middleton

Ca

Wardlow

Burbage

BUXTON

Wormhill

Millers Dale

Cressbrook

Little Longstone

Rowland

Goyt's Moss

Cat and Fiddle

Blackwell

River Wye

Monsal Head

Great Longstone

A54

Harpur Hill

King Sterndale

A5270

Taddington

Chelmorton

Ashford in the Water

12

A6020

A619

A54

Brand Si

Sheldon

BAKEWELL

A6

Contains Ordnance Survey Data © Crown Copyright and Database Right.

/ CONTENTS

THE ROUTES

ROUTE GRADES

Easy	●○○○
Medium	●●○○
Hard	●●●○

/ INTRODUCTION

Kinder Scout is a mountain to return to time and time again, with routes around the foothills, up its cloughs and on its plateau. This collection aims to offer you plenty of options so that you can choose a walk to suit the weather, your fitness or how many sandwiches you can fit in your rucksack. The routes highlight notable landmarks and wildlife to encourage you to pause and connect with this remarkable landscape.

Rather than being a peak-shaped mountain, Kinder Scout is characterised by its large central moorland plateau. Reaching its rocky edges can feel like a hard climb, but it's worth the effort once you're walking along them, enjoying the expansive views around you. Kinder Scout is the highest point in the Peak District, and you can see Manchester from the western edges, Bleaklow and Alport Castles from the northern edges, and the beautiful Hope Valley and beyond from the southern and eastern edges. On a really clear day you can see as far as the mountains of Eryri (Snowdonia) in Wales.

You can expect to encounter many fascinating geological features here, including wind-carved rock formations and exposed tors. Kinder Scout is situated in the Dark Peak area, which is characterised by dark-toned gritstone laid down between 360 and 300 million years ago when the area was a vast river delta. It contrasts dramatically with the White Peak in the southern Peak District, where the gritstone has eroded away, leaving light grey limestone rocks visible on the surface.

Although you will become well acquainted with bogs on some of these walks, the black peat is much less exposed these days thanks to the work of the Moors For The Future Partnership (***www.moorsforthefuture.org.uk***) to restore and conserve blanket bogs across the Peak District. The results include an increase in biodiversity and the restoration of many moorland bird habitats, improvements in water quality, and reduced flood risk downstream. Curlews, golden plovers and dippers are just some of the birds that you'll hear or see in the area.

I predict that these walking routes will merely whet your appetite for Kinder Scout as it has a habit of drawing people back in.

Sarah Lister

Purple heather on Ringing Roger in summer.

ACKNOWLEDGEMENTS

'Kinder has so many different moods. You could go up twenty, thirty days and each one would be different.' (Gordon Miller)

This guidebook is dedicated to Gordon Miller (1941–2023) who passionately shared his knowledge and love of Kinder Scout by connecting with people through his work as a warden and ranger, and through elaborate storytelling in the pub.

Heartfelt thanks to Clare Kelly for recceing some of the walks with me, and to everyone who has encouraged and supported me along the way, with special mention to: John Beatty, Paul Besley, Zak Wolstenholme and his family, Ali Foxon, Jon Hyde, Chris Reid at the Penny Pot Cafe, Jen Scotney, Hanna Varga, Sara Moeskjaer and Wayne Fallon. Thank you with a hug! I'd also like to add a giant thank you to Jon Barton who offered me the opportunity in the first place, plus everyone at Vertebrate who has worked on the book.

ABOUT THE WALKS

Most of the walks in this book begin from Edale which is on the Hope Valley railway line between Sheffield and Manchester. Others start from the village of Hayfield, and from the Snake Pass. Edale and Hayfield are both well-equipped villages with pubs, cafes and public toilets. For the walk up Fair Brook from the Snake Pass you'll need to be extra prepared as there are no facilities other than parking.

The Countryside and Rights of Way Act of 2000 (CRoW Act, sometimes referred to as the 'right to roam') came into effect in England in October 2005, and this granted legal access for those on foot to enjoy exploring 'access land'. Given that there are also a huge number of historical public rights of way (public footpaths or bridleways) within and outside the access land, there is a wealth of terrain to enjoy and explore in this area.

For clarity, ease of use and planning, the walks described in this guidebook usually follow established public rights of way, where you have the legal right to 'pass and repass along the way'. Some of the routes use permissive paths, where a landowner has granted access, but this is not defined by law and walkers must adhere to waymarkers or signs placed by the landowner (for example, the National Trust, which acquired Kinder Scout in 1982). The walk sections in upland terrain mostly follow established paths across CRoW access land and some of these routes are clearer than others on the ground, depending on their popularity. Some routes across access land are mapped and some are not; this may also depend on what type of mapping you're using.

The timings quoted for each walk are quite generous, assuming an average walking pace of 3–4km/h (2–3mph), which also factors in time for short breaks, photos and the effort of ascent/terrain as applicable. The 'running' times quoted reflect the fact that a runner may move more efficiently over most terrain, but will still walk many of the ascents, moving at an average speed of 5–8km/h (3–5mph).

NAVIGATION

The mapping and descriptions in this guidebook are intended for planning and information; you will need to use additional mapping and navigation methods while walking, either a hard-copy map and compass, or good quality online mapping app (such as OS Maps, Gaia GPS, OutdoorActive or Topo GPS) on a mobile phone or GPS unit. Both require practice; understanding maps and symbols and orienting yourself from them is a useful skill to learn; there are many tutorial videos online that can help with this.

While many mountain users access route and mapping information on mobile devices or GPS units, be aware that digital mapping sources can drain your mobile phone/GPS unit's battery; make sure that you carry a hard-copy map which does not rely on having mobile phone signal and will increase your ability to see the bigger picture. Pack a portable power bank to recharge your device on the hill, especially if you also want to use your phone to make calls or take photos.

Using a map and compass will increase your accuracy and confidence when navigating in poor visibility, especially on the plateau where there are very few features other than boulders and cairns. Understandably, many walkers get disoriented on Kinder Scout plateau but this can be avoided by checking your location and direction of travel before walking in completely the wrong direction. It's best not to make assumptions while you're up there: find out your location, check the direction of travel, and always take a torch and mobile phone with spare batteries.

The walks all appear on the following maps:
- **Ordnance Survey Explorer OL1 The Peak District: Dark Peak – 1:25,000**
  A large-scale map suitable for walking with lots of detail. Four centimetres on the map represent one kilometre in real life. These maps come in a paper or weatherproof laminated format and come with a link to a digital version to use in the OS Maps app.
- **Harvey Maps/BMC British Mountain Map Dark Peak – 1:40,000**
  This map is slightly smaller scale, but is excellent for walking and planning routes, due to the visual use of colours to denote mountain heights/terrain. Two and a half centimetres on the map represent one kilometre in real life. These maps are printed on waterproof paper and are very light to carry. This map includes a detailed enlargement of the Kinder plateau.

SAFETY & WELL-BEING

Keeping safe and well in upland terrain starts with an appropriate plan that suits both you and your group and the forecast weather and mountain conditions, and allows for enjoyment and adventure along the way. Bear in mind that a robust plan will allow for changes; you shouldn't be locked into a single objective, as outside factors may influence your day. These factors might include changeable weather and how it affects you on the hill, how you/the group are feeling given the terrain or effort, your estimated/actual speed of travel, the length of daylight hours, parking and access/public transport times, what clothing you're wearing/carrying and even how much food/drink you have with you. Let someone outside your group know where you're going and what time you're expecting to be back down (and let them know when you're off the hill to prevent them from worrying). When planning your day, check out ***www.adventuresmart.uk*** for helpful tips and reminders of what factors to consider. *#BeAdventureSmart*

If you're unsure about aspects of your planned route, do some research online to find out more or ask for advice in local accommodation or shops to fill your knowledge gaps. Ensure that you have enough protective clothing and equipment for the forecast weather and get an updated forecast appropriate for your planned route. The Met Office provides a mountain highpoint forecast for Kinder Low which will usually be very different to valley level weather, since the air is colder the higher you ascend. Check the weather forecast for the valleys, such as Edale, and the high points such as Kinder Low and Mam Tor, to prepare adequately for the conditions. Remember that conditions can change quickly so it is usually worth packing extra layers and waterproofs.

Don't underestimate how much food and drink you might need for longer/ higher outings, especially when walking with children. Plan to snack/drink every 30 to 40 minutes to keep energy levels high and avoid tired limbs or slowing down. The walking times in this guidebook include some time to stop to eat or drink, but always keep an eye on your walking pace and how this compares to your plans. Are the weather conditions or terrain affecting your speed? Do you still have time to complete your planned objective or should you shorten your route or turn back earlier than planned? Never be afraid to check on your group, check your map, check your watch and change plans if necessary, especially if you can see or feel bad weather arriving quicker than forecasted.

KIT & COMFORT

When choosing clothes and kit for mountain walks, think about the principles of comfort and protection. Avoid cotton clothing, as these lose their insulating properties when damp with sweat or wet with rain. Comfortable, synthetic walking trousers or leggings are a good option, as is a synthetic top or base layer over which a warm layer can be added. Don't forget to protect your arms, head and neck in very sunny weather.

Take a rucksack containing an extra warm layer (or two if it's very cold), a pair of warm gloves and a hat, a zippable, waterproof jacket with a large hood, and waterproof trousers that you can pull over your walking trousers/leggings. Layering several thinner layers is more flexible than wearing a very thick ski jacket or similar.

Your rucksack should also contain food, drink, a map, a phone charger and power bank, and a waterproof bag to keep everything in. You might also wish to include a head torch (and spare batteries), depending on the time of year/time of day that you're planning to walk, a small first aid kit, and an emergency group shelter that you can sit on or in for lunch breaks or use for emergency shelter in the event of an unforeseen situation or injury. When packing your kit, ask yourself 'Can I keep myself comfortable, warm and dry even if I'm walking much more slowly than planned or if I've stopped completely, in a variety of weather and mountain conditions?'

For some of the routes, a pair of trail/off-road trainers with an aggressive sole may be sufficient; it is best to avoid flat-soled trainers as these don't provide enough grip on rock or in wet conditions. Walking boots offer good ankle support and excellent grip, but make sure you get used to wearing them before a long day out.

Ticks can carry Lyme disease; they lurk in the bracken and long vegetation in summer so walking trousers are advised during this season. Walk in the middle of paths and avoid unnecessarily walking through bushy vegetation or long grass. Advice for preventing tick bites and tick removal is available here: **www.lymediseaseaction.org.uk**

Check a mountain weather forecast to ensure that you pack the kit you need (including precautionary extras) and make sure you wear a watch so you can keep track of time. Always 'Stop and Be Bothered' to change/add a layer rather than ignoring what your body or the weather are telling you.

/ MOUNTAIN RESCUE

Mountain Rescue England and Wales is a charity that relies on volunteer time, donations and fundraising to operate. The walks covered in this guidebook are located in Edale, Hayfield, the Snake Pass and Kinder Scout, which are covered by the Kinder Mountain Rescue Team, Edale Mountain Rescue Team and Glossop Mountain Rescue Team. Visit **www.mountain.rescue.org.uk** for more information.

Many mountain rescue calls are made when people find themselves in exposed conditions in poor weather or darkness, lost, or overcome by fatigue or cold/wet/hot weather. Making appropriate plans and amending them if needed, as well as eating adequate food and taking enough kit, clothing and mapping will help to safeguard against things unravelling during the day.

That said, mountain rescue teams advise that you should always call if you need assistance. They can sometimes provide advice over the telephone to help you take the best action on the hill for you and your group.

What To Do in an Emergency

If you or someone else is in need of emergency assistance in the mountains, dial **999** (or **112**) and ask for **POLICE** and then **MOUNTAIN RESCUE**. This relies on you having mobile phone signal and a charged phone battery, and being able to give the relevant details over the phone when asked (location, name/s and details of people affected, what has happened and your contact details). You may be asked to stay in position or in signal range so the mountain rescue team can call you back. Keep yourself and others warm and insulated from the ground and the weather. Put on layers, eat something for energy and sit out of the wind on a bag or clothing.

Emergency Rescue By SMS Text

In the UK you can contact the emergency services by SMS text. While this service is primarily intended for those with hearing or speech difficulties, it can be useful if you have low battery or intermittent signal. You need to register your phone beforehand by texting '**register**' to **999** and then following the instructions in the reply. ***www.emergencysms.net***

| BEHAVIOUR & RESPECTING THE ENVIRONMENT

Due to the popularity of Kinder Scout and its surrounding areas, it is imperative that you take the time to plan visits to maximise enjoyment and safety, and avoid having a negative impact on the natural environment and local communities. During busy holiday times, it is usually inconsiderate parking, inappropriate behaviour in public spaces (shouting, loud music, taking illegal drugs) and discarded food remains/litter that create the highest impact, as well as dogs causing worry or injury to local livestock. These problems can all be ameliorated by modifying your behaviour and attitudes in the light of the surrounding communities and landscape. For further information, see ***www.peakdistrict.gov.uk/visiting/planning-your-visit/countryside-code***

A summary of the Countryside Code is below:
Respect everyone
- be considerate to those living in, working in and enjoying the countryside
- leave gates and property as you find them
- do not block access to gateways or driveways when parking

- be nice, say hello, share the space
- follow local signs and keep to marked paths unless wider access is available

Protect the environment
- take your litter home – leave no trace of your visit (including fruit peel, sanitary items, nappies, dog poo bags, tissue paper)
- do not light fires and only have BBQs where signs say you can
- always keep your dogs under control and in sight
- dog poo – bag it and bin it in any public waste bin or take it home
- care for nature – do not cause damage or disturbance (no fires, do not move stones, damage ruins or plants and trees, or disturb wildlife)

Enjoy the outdoors
- check your route (make sure you have the relevant maps) and local conditions
- plan your adventure – know what to expect and what you can do
- enjoy your visit, have fun, make a memory

Know the signs and symbols of the countryside
- Public Footpath, Public Bridleway
- Restricted Byway, Byway Open to All Traffic, Permissive Path
- Open Access Land, End of Open Access Land

| WALKING WITH YOUR DOG

Shared adventures with our canine companions can be wonderful. However, given the delicate balance between outdoor recreation and farming around Kinder Scout, it's essential to know how to look after our dogs, both for their health and safety and for the wellbeing of other people and animals around us, including grazing livestock and local wildlife.

Legally on a Public Right of Way an owner does not have to keep a dog on a lead, as long as the dog remains under 'close control'. However, the advice from Peak District National Park is to keep dogs on a short lead. On Open Access Land, there is a legal requirement to keep dogs on a short lead between 1 March and 31 July to safeguard breeding ground nesting birds and livestock, and owners must always be in control of their dog. Farmers have the legal right to destroy any dog that is causing worry or harm to livestock.

Dog poo needs to be bagged up and disposed of in an appropriate bin as it can contain bacteria and parasites which are a health risk to grazing animals, people and dogs. There are not any bins provided on or around Kinder Scout, so all litter and waste will need to be disposed of in Edale or Hayfield where bins are provided, or taken home with you.

Be wary of how your dog will behave around livestock. Keep your distance from cows and horses where possible, especially if the animals have their young with them. If animals closely follow or chase you, let go of your dog's lead and focus on your own safety.

| HOW TO USE THIS BOOK

Use this book for inspiration, to improve your knowledge, find out local information and as part of your planning process. The maps in this book are the same as the Ordnance Survey Explorer OL1 map described on page ix, but you should always take a separate map out with you in case you need to refer to the wider area around the walk. The text descriptions allow you to work your way through the route visually with a map before you set out, as well as providing a reference when you're walking. Familiarise yourself with the symbols used on the map and consider possible escape routes in case you need to retrace your steps or lose height to escape poor weather.

The descriptions of the routes in the Mountains Walks series as …

Easy	●○○○
Medium	●●○○
Hard	●●●○
Full-on	●●●● (No routes with this rating in this book.)

… do not just relate to the distance of the route. The gradings have been reached by considering a mixture of distance, ascent profile, type of terrain and technicality and how easy the route might be to navigate in poor weather.

Follow the advice above about choosing equipment, using mountain-specific weather forecasts and how to look after yourself and your party to maximise your enjoyment and safety. Additional information can be found via the websites listed, which offer further opportunities to increase your knowledge and confidence in planning and enjoying walks in the mountainous terrain on and around Kinder Scout.

Map Key

S	**2**	↗	**52**
Route starting point	**Route marker**	**Direction arrow**	**Additional grid line numbers to aid navigation**

| GLOSSARY

Booth – a small settlement which was originally used as a location for temporary shelter by shepherds tending cattle during the summer.

Cairn – a heap of stones found on some summits and at key junctions along routes. They are mostly used as markers, but sometimes built as memorials. Some are carefully arranged; others are loosely piled up.

Cascade – a series of shallow waterfalls.

Clough – a gorge or narrow steep-sided ravine.

Dipper – a short-tailed bird with a white throat and breast often found in fast-flowing rivers. They feed on aquatic invertebrates plucked from the bottoms of streams and riverbeds. They have a third, transparent eyelid that they can close, enabling them to see underwater.

Flagged path – A path covered with large, flat, square pieces of stone.

Grough – a natural channel or opening in a peat moor.

Hag – a type of erosion at the sides of gullies as a result of water flow eroding downwards into the peat or where a fire or overgrazing has exposed the peat surface to dry out and blow or wash away. They appear as isolated slabs or overhanging banks of peat.

Jagger – someone who owned/led a team of packhorses that were historically used to carry goods across long distances for trade.

Knoll – a small rounded hill or mound.

Packhorse – a horse that carries goods on its back.

Pasture – land covered with grass and other low plants suitable for grazing animals, especially cattle or sheep.

Trigpoint or *trig* – the common name for 'triangulation pillars' – concrete pillars, about four feet tall, which were used by the Ordnance Survey (OS) to re-map Britain. They appear on OS maps as a blue triangle with a dot in the middle.

3.5km / 2.2 miles

01 / PICNIC & PADDLE ALONG GRINDS BROOK

A short valley walk from Edale village to Grinds Brook for a picnic on the riverbank and a paddle in the water.

/ ESSENTIAL INFO

GRADE ●○○○

DISTANCE **3.5KM/2.2 MILES**

ASCENT **116M**

TIME **1.5 HRS (WALKER)/30 MINS (RUNNER)**

START/FINISH **EDALE**

START GRID REF **SK 123 853**

START GPS **53.3648, -1.8160**

OS MAP **OL1 THE PEAK DISTRICT: DARK PEAK AREA (1:25,000)**

/ OVERVIEW

This is the perfect introduction to Kinder Scout in summer – a stunning valley walk on which to watch the wildlife, refresh your feet in the cool water, and share a picnic with friends or family. The route passes through open pasture with incredible views up to the bouldery southern edges of Kinder Scout plateau, then continues through a small woodland with a couple of shady benches where you might see grey squirrels or hear the cuckoo calling. At Golden Clough there is a beautiful arched wooden bridge which makes a special photograph. Soon after you drop down to the riverbank where you can easily while away a few hours watching the dippers and enjoying a paddle, before returning to Edale village for an ice cream.

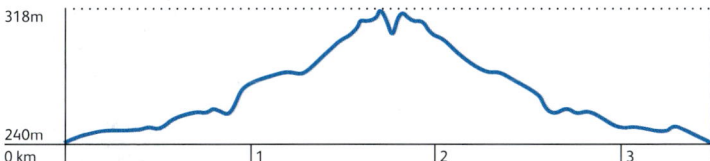

Looking up to Ringing Roger from Golden Clough and Grinds Brook.

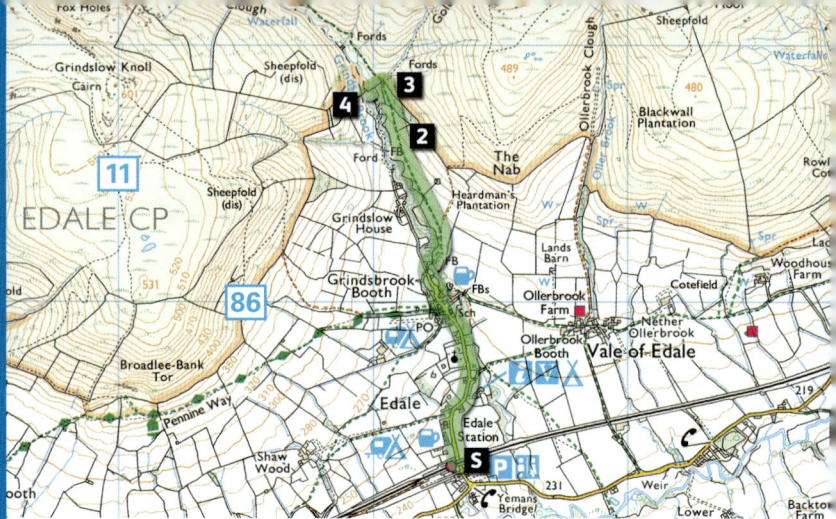

| DIRECTIONS

S From underneath the railway bridge on the road into Edale village, head up into the village. Pass the visitor centre on your right and the church on your left. About 100m after the Old Nags Head pub the road changes from tarmac to unsurfaced track. A short distance further on, immediately before white iron gates, a footpath is signed right into the woods – **take this**, cross the river over the footbridge, then climb out the other side and follow the paved path into open pasture alongside the woods.

2 After 600m go through the gate into a small woodland. There's a bench on the right where it's nice to take a breather in the shade and listen out for the cuckoo in summer. Walk through the woodland and go through the next gate.

3 **Turn left** after the gate and walk down the steps and cross the wooden arched bridge at Golden Clough. **Turn left** after the bridge to follow the steps up (SK 120 868), then immediately **turn left** to walk down to Grinds Brook where there are sections of riverbank to sit for a picnic and a paddle. If it's busy there are more riverbank areas further up the brook which can be reached either by walking along the water's edge or by rejoining the footpath and dropping back down further along. The next best place to drop down to the riverbank is 200m from Golden Clough bridge after the next ford and trees (SK 119 870) – it's a bit steep to walk down but is a nice spot with a cascade.

4 Simply retrace your steps to return to Edale village for refreshments and public toilets. Remember to take all of your waste with you.

/ GOOD TO KNOW

Edale sits on the Manchester–Sheffield railway line and is well served by trains daily.

There are pay & display car parks in Edale village and at the station – these can fill up early on fine weather weekends.

This is a very enjoyable walk and is a good option throughout the year, but for picnic and paddling purposes it's best in late spring and summer. In May and June there are cuckoos calling from the trees, foxgloves flowering among the ferns and bees buzzing in the hawthorn blossom. In August and September there is the purple haze of heather, and bilberries to snack on – if the sheep don't eat them first. Listen and look for birds too: stonechats, buzzards and dippers.

The first section up to the woodland is flagged, then the path becomes rougher with small loose rocks and tree roots so

watch your step. There is a short, steep section from the bridge down to the riverbank. Navigation is straightforward.

There are toilets at the car park and at the Edale visitor centre. The visitor centre also has a shop and can provide local information; it's next to the Fieldhead Campsite. The Penny Pot Cafe by Edale station is perfectly placed for pre- or post-walk refreshments. There's also a cafe at Newfold Farm further into the village, as well as a general store. There are a couple of pubs in the village – the Rambler Inn and the Old Nags Head.

Livestock and ground-nesting birds mean the Kinder area is a dog-on-lead kind of place, particularly between 1 March and 31 July when it is the law under the CRoW Act that dogs must be on short leads.

This is a fun choice for young kids that like to play in the water. The water is shallow but the rocks in the river can be slippery so care

should be taken and ideally water shoes worn.

All litter, including dog waste, must be carried back to the village or taken home with you for disposal. There are bins opposite the school. BBQs and fires are forbidden as they damage the moorland environment and often cause wildfires.

In September 1955 a Rescue Post was established at the Old Nags Head pub which became the first Edale Mountain Rescue base; its first exercise took place on 19 February 1956.

Bilberries grow on low bushes with solitary blue-black fruits; they are similar to blueberries, but have red rather than white flesh inside. They have a number of different names across geographical regions including blaeberry in Scotland, whortleberry, wimberry and whinberry.

Dippers can be seen all year round, and are often spotted bobbing up and down on a stone in a river or stream. They can see underwater to help them catch underwater invertebrates.

5.5km / 3.4 miles

02 / BOOTHS & BRIDGES VALLEY WALK

An easy low-level walk from Edale along the start of the Pennine Way to Upper Booth Farm, returning to the village through open pasture.

/ ESSENTIAL INFO

GRADE ●●○○○

DISTANCE **5.5KM/3.4 MILES**

ASCENT **138M**

TIME **1.5 HRS (WALKER)/45 MINS (RUNNER)**

START/FINISH **EDALE**

START GRID REF **SK 123 853**

START GPS **53.3648, -1.8160**

OS MAP **OL1 THE PEAK DISTRICT: DARK PEAK AREA (1:25,000)**

/ OVERVIEW

Experience the start of the Pennine Way, spot wildlife in the Edale Valley, walk through the historical 'booths' which used to be herdsman's shelters, and watch trains pass through the Hope Valley. This picturesque route climbs gently and steadily out of Grindsbrook Booth, before dropping down to Upper Booth and joining a path through open pasture to Barber Booth. In spring and summer you may have the opportunity to hear and see wild birds along the way, including curlews and peewits. In good weather you can enjoy views up to Kinder Scout and the Mam Tor ridge. From here, the walk returns to Edale train station or the car park and, conveniently, the Penny Pot Cafe.

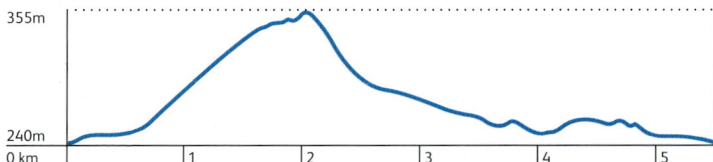

Approaching Upper Booth.

Fingerpost marking the start of the Pennine Way.

/ DIRECTIONS

S From underneath the railway bridge on the road into Edale village, head up into the village. Pass the visitor centre on your right and the church on your left. A short distance further on, immediately before reaching the Old Nags Head, the Pennine Way is signed to the **left** on a fingerpost – take this tree-lined footpath alongside a stream.

2 After 300m the path splits. **Take the left** through the gate, following the signposted Pennine Way. **Keep going** for 900m through open pasture and listen out for the call of the curlew if you're walking this route in the spring or summer. There's a good bench along the way with views to Mam Tor ridge.

3 After going through a gate the path briefly ascends more steeply. **Keep straight on**, walking towards a drystone wall with a gate in the middle. Go through the gate and descend the path that winds between two hillocks. After another gate you will pass a ruined farm building on your left. Continue along the rough track towards the farm and houses at Upper Booth.

4 At the end of the rough track, go through the gate that brings you to a T-junction. **Turn left** along the lane. There's a signpost almost immediately on the right (SK 103 853), before reaching the farm and outbuildings. This is where you leave the Pennine Way. **Take the sharp left**, marked as a *Public Footpath* on the signpost.

Friendly gatekeepers at the start of the Pennine Way.

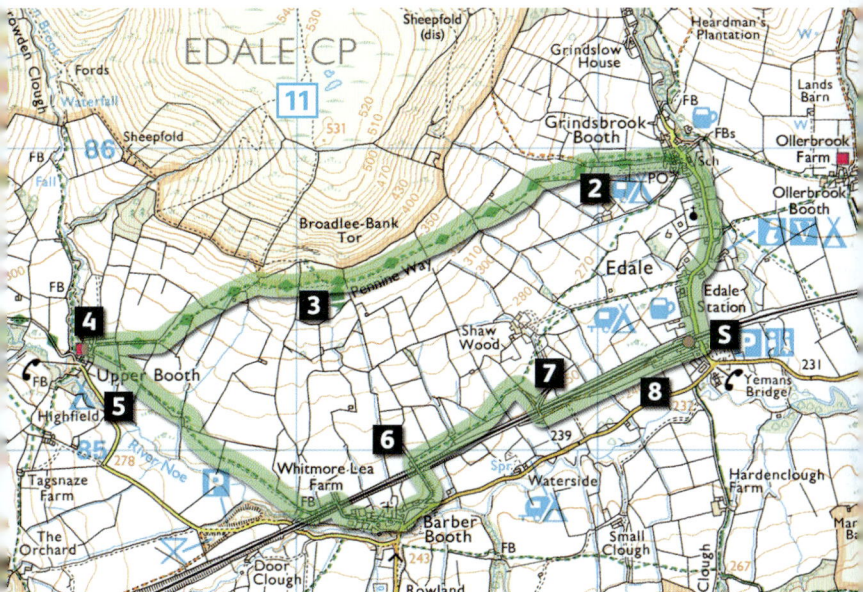

Approaching sunset near the start of the Pennine Way.

5 As you walk through the fields, which often have livestock in them, you'll cross two short stone bridges, a wooden bridge, and a larger railway bridge that takes you into the hamlet of Barber Booth. Follow the track through the farm buildings and houses of Barber Booth. Shortly after passing a Methodist chapel on the left, the track meets a T-junction. **Turn left** to walk along the lane for about 80m, then **turn left** to join the signposted track.

6 After crossing the railway bridge, **turn right** through a gate and follow the path. After the next gate, follow the path to the **right** alongside the edge of the field parallel with the train tracks. Continue on the path through more fields until you reach a signposted concession path. **Take the right turn** towards Edale Station.

7 After going through a couple of gates to meet a gravel track, continue on to cross the railway bridge and follow the bend to the left. When the gravel track meets a field, follow the signposted path towards Edale station across the field, walking parallel to the train tracks now on your left.

8 On meeting a short wooden fence at the end of the path, **turn left** to go through a gate into a small woodland, then almost immediately **turn right** to walk towards Edale station car park. If you have time for a brew or an ice cream, the Penny Pot Cafe is conveniently located just past Edale station entrance. To get to the main car park, **turn right** after the Penny Pot Cafe and cross the road to the car park.

GOOD TO KNOW

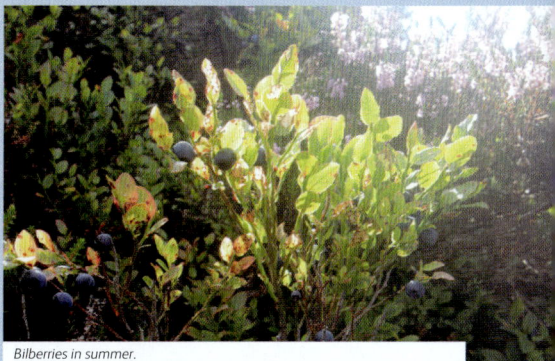
Bilberries in summer.

Edale sits on the Manchester–Sheffield railway line and is well served by trains daily.

There are pay & display car parks in Edale village and at the station. These can fill up early on fine weather weekends. The Edale Valley is situated just north of the Hope Valley and is easily accessible from the main A6187 road in Hope or from Mam Nick on the Rushup Edge road west of Mam Tor.

WHEN TO WALK IT

This is a great outing all year round in good weather. It can be very muddy after prolonged periods of rain so put boots on rather than your best trainers. Some of it is flagstoned but there are often large patches of soggy pastureland.

TERRAIN AND NAVIGATION

There are some uneven paths and muddy sections. The route is not accessible for wheelchairs or prams/pushchairs. The route is well signposted.

FACILITIES AND REFRESHMENTS

There are toilets at the car park and at the Edale visitor centre. The visitor centre also has a shop and can provide local information; it's next to the Fieldhead Campsite. The Penny Pot Cafe by Edale station is perfectly placed for pre- or post-walk refreshments. There's also a cafe at Newfold Farm further into the village, as well as a general store. There are also a couple of pubs in the village – the Rambler Inn and the Old Nags Head.

DOGS AND KIDS

Livestock and ground-nesting birds mean that dogs need to be on a lead, particularly between 1 March and 31 July when it is the law under the CRoW Act that dogs must be on short leads. The fields often contain livestock.

This is a family friendly route which only takes up a fraction of the day, so it's a good choice for a half-day visit with young children. Then you could drive on to Castleton via Mam Nick and the limestone gorge of Winnats Pass to visit one of the caverns.

POINTS OF INTEREST

Edale village is the starting point for the historic 268-mile Pennine Way which runs to Kirk Yetholm. It was the first National Trail in England when it was opened in 1965.

Barber Booth is one of the original booths (vaccaries or cattle farms) of Edale and dates from when the area was part of the Royal Forest – a royal hunting forest established by the Normans.

Mam Tor is the site of one of the earliest hill forts in Britain and is protected as a scheduled monument.

4.5km / 2.8 miles

03 / OLLER BROOK & THE NAB

A short but moderately high circular walk from Edale up on to the The Nab via Ollerbrook Clough; a good one for wildlife watching.

| ESSENTIAL INFO

GRADE ● ● ○ ○
DISTANCE **4.5KM/2.8 MILES**
ASCENT **212M**
TIME **1.5 HRS (WALKER)/40 MINS (RUNNER)**
START/FINISH **EDALE**
START GRID REF **SK 123 853**
START GPS **53.3648, -1.8160**
OS MAP **OL1 THE PEAK DISTRICT: DARK PEAK AREA (1:25,000)**

| OVERVIEW

Although this is a relatively short walk, the rewards are high. Peaceful and abounding in wildlife in spring and summer, you may hear ring ouzels or stonechats in the early morning, and see bees and butterflies. There are plenty of sheep with their lambs in spring too! The route climbs gradually up to the rocky crest of The Nab, which offers a fantastic view of Edale village below with Mam Tor ridge as a backdrop to the south, and of the Kinder Scout plateau in all other directions! Definitely a good spot for some panorama shots and a picnic. From here it zigzags steeply down towards Grinds Brook before dropping you back into Edale.

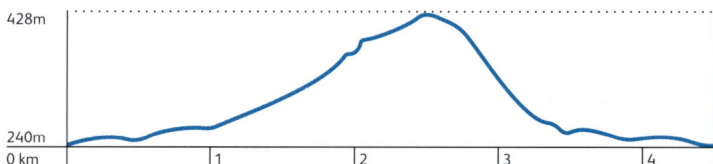

View to Kinder Scout from Oller Brook.

Autumn mist over Ollerbrook Booth.

| DIRECTIONS

S From underneath the railway bridge on the road into Edale village, head up into the village. Pass the Rambler Inn pub on the left and the Fieldhead Campsite on the right. Immediately after the campsite grounds there is a footpath signed to the right into the woods next to a small cemetery – take **this lane**, go through the gate and follow the track **straight ahead (north-east)** into open pasture.

2 Go through the next gate to continue along the track towards Ollerbrook Farm. Walk into the farmyard and **turn right**, passing more outbuildings and some cottages.

3 At the crossroads (SK 128 859) **turn left** to go past a small residential parking area and through a small gate into open pasture. Follow the grassy path round to the right to walk parallel with the stream – Oller Brook. This path trends gently uphill and goes through four gates. Listen and look out for wildlife along Oller Brook as this is often a quieter area of the valley.

4 After the fourth gate, the path splits. **Continue in the same direction, heading north** for about 200m then following the path round to the left, heading south-west for 450m to the crest of The Nab. Walk over to its rocky outcrop for seriously impressive views (in good weather). Kinder Scout plateau towers behind you, Mam Tor ridge ahead of you, and what can you spot in Edale village below? Perhaps the church tower or the pubs? This is a great spot for a picnic or a flask of tea and quality thinking time.

View to Back Tor and Mam Tor ridge from The Nab.

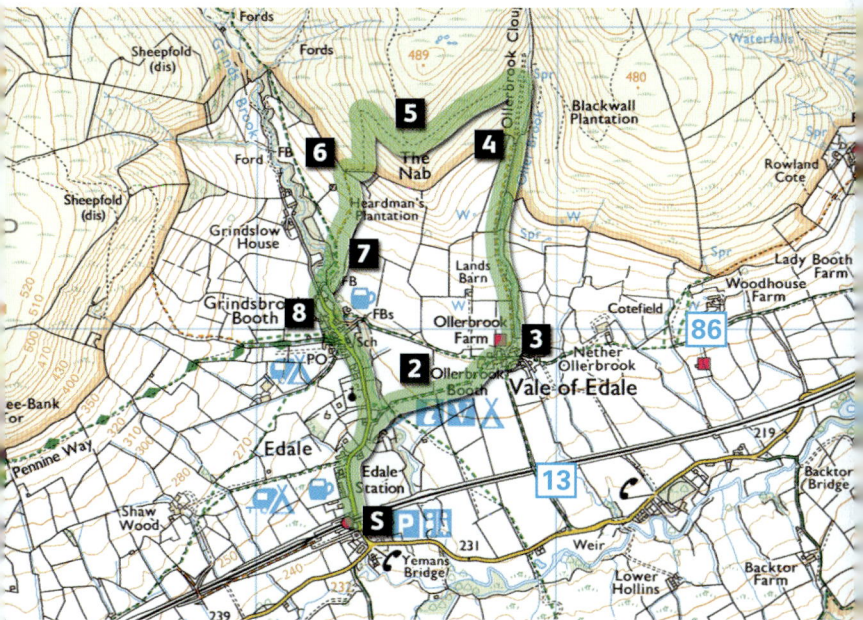

View to Grindslow Knoll from The Nab.

5 From here, head north-west, following the edge of the crest towards a footpath junction (SK 124 866). **Take the left path downhill.** The first section has loose stones and small rocks, then becomes stepped as it steeply zigzags down past a small tree plantation to a gate.

6 After the gate, follow the rough path down into open pasture. This path has loose stones to begin with, then becomes grassy as it descends towards a stone guidepost and a flagged footpath.

7 **Turn left** on to the flagged footpath, passing a small stone barn. At the end of the flagged path, follow the steps down to a gate. After the gate, cross the footbridge and follow steps up to a lane and a cottage.

8 **Turn left** on to the lane to walk into Grindsbrook Booth in Edale village. The nearest pub is the Old Nags Head and the nearest cafe is at Newfold, where there's also a general store. Follow the road down to the car parks and train station, close to the Rambler Inn pub and the Penny Pot Cafe. Take your pick!

/ GOOD TO KNOW

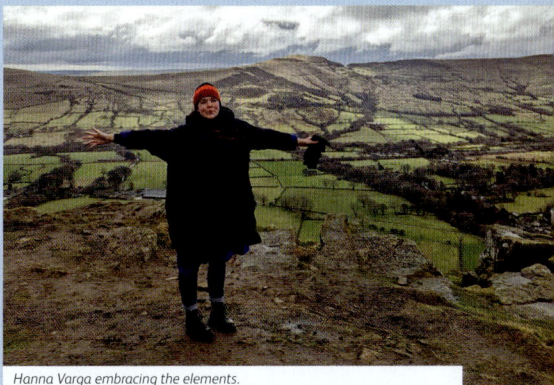
Hanna Varga embracing the elements.

PUBLIC TRANSPORT AND ACCESS

Edale sits on the Manchester–Sheffield railway line and is well served by trains daily.

There are pay & display car parks in Edale village and at the station; these can fill up early on fine weekends. The Edale Valley is situated just north of the Hope Valley and is easily accessible from the main A6187 road in Hope, or from Mam Nick on the Rushup Edge road west of Mam Tor.

WHEN TO WALK IT

This is a great route all year round. There is more wildlife to see in spring and summer, and during August and September there is an abundance of bilberries and purple heather.

TERRAIN AND NAVIGATION

There are steep paths and rocky sections on the ascent and descent. Navigation is straightforward but it is advisable to carry a map and compass, and to know how to use them.

FACILITIES AND REFRESHMENTS

There are toilets at the car park and at the Edale visitor centre. The visitor centre also has a shop and can provide local information; it's next to the Fieldhead Campsite. The Penny Pot Cafe by Edale station is perfectly placed for pre- or post-walk refreshments. There's also a cafe at Newfold Farm further into the village, as well as a general store. There are a couple of pubs in the village – the Rambler Inn and the Old Nags Head.

DOGS AND KIDS

Livestock and ground-nesting birds mean Kinder is a dog-on-lead kind of place, particularly between 1 March and 31 July when it is the law under the CRoW Act that dogs must be on short leads.

This walk is suitable for active kids, who will enjoy seeing the sheep and lambs when they are out in the fields. You could make it into a longer day out by turning right at the footpath along Grinds Brook, then dropping down to the brook after crossing the pretty arched bridge (page 1). There are plenty of places for a paddle and a picnic.

POINTS OF INTEREST

Ring ouzels breed on the upland moors and rocky crags in summer. Males sing from prominent crags and boulders such as those towering over Oller Brook.

Stonechats are a small bird that inhabit the heaths along Oller Brook and can be identified by their call, which sounds like two small stones being hit together.

7km / 4.3 miles

04 / CROWDEN BROOK WOODLAND WALK

A low-level circular walk from Edale to Crowden Brook valley, passing beautiful cascades and including a woodland section.

/ ESSENTIAL INFO

GRADE ●●○○○
DISTANCE **7KM/4.3 MILES**
ASCENT **220M**
TIME **2.5 HRS (WALKER)/1.5 HRS (RUNNER)**
START/FINISH **EDALE**
START GRID REF **SK 123 853**
START GPS **53.3648, -1.8160**
OS MAP **OL1 THE PEAK DISTRICT: DARK PEAK AREA (1:25,000)**

/ OVERVIEW

Crowden Brook is a relatively quiet area of Kinder Scout, offering excellent views up to the boulders of Crowden Tower at the top of the clough. This route begins fairly gently out of Edale along the start of the Pennine Way, then climbs slightly to join the narrow hillside path of Broadlee-Bank towards Crowden Brook. For quite a small effort, the view of Crowden Clough really is special from this valley. From here, it follows the course of the brook downhill through woodlands and passing cascades before reaching Upper Booth and returning you to Edale through open pasture. Best enjoyed in spring when the wild flowers are in bloom, including bluebells and foxgloves, or in autumn when the fungi is flourishing.

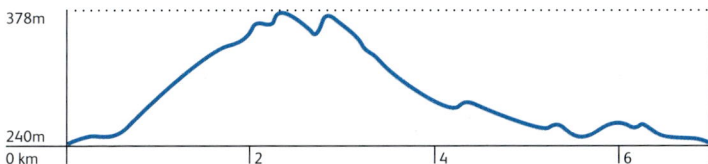

Looking up Crowden Clough to Kinder Scout.

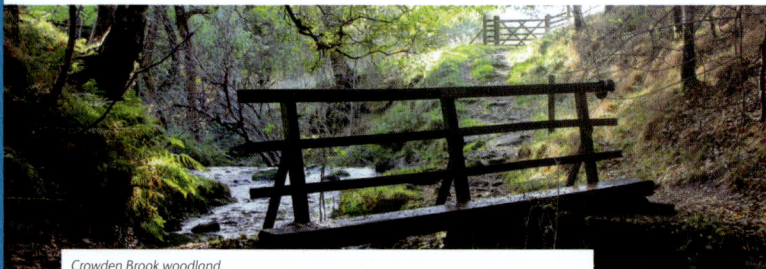
Crowden Brook woodland.

❘ DIRECTIONS

S From underneath the railway bridge on the road into Edale village, head up into the village. Pass the visitor centre on your right and the church on your left. A short distance further on, immediately before reaching the Old Nags Head, the Pennine Way is signed left on a fingerpost – **turn left** along the tree-lined footpath beside a stream.

2 After 300m the path splits. **Take the left fork** through the gate, signposted *Pennine Way*. Keep going for 900m through open pasture and listen out for the call of the curlew if you're walking this route in the spring or summer. There's a good bench for a sit-down along the way with a superb view of Mam Tor ridge.

3 After going through a gate the path begins to ascend more steeply and splits (SK 111 855). **Turn right** along the grassy path, towards a wooden fence and gate. Go through the gate, **turn left** and follow the narrow path that curves around the foothill of Broadlee-Bank Tor for 650m (ignore the steep uphill paths to your right). On reaching a small private woodland behind a stone wall, continue on the same path down to a narrow brook (which may or may not have water flowing). Cross the brook and go through the gate to walk uphill for a short distance. Continue along the path as it levels out through a small tree plantation area and towards a large wooden gate. After going through the gate, continue along the path for 350m. (Note the path can be tricky to see in summer due to the growth of ferns.)

4 Just before reaching a narrow brook, there's a faint trod to the **left** (SK 102 862) that leads down to a wider path. Take this, then **turn left** on to the wider path and follow this for 250m, going through a gate next to a National Trust sign-post for *Crowden Clough* on the way. Go through the next gate into the small woodland – there is a lovely shaded area to the right if you need a pit stop. Then cross the footbridge and **turn left** to go through a large wooden gate that leads into open pasture. Follow the grassy path for 250m and look out for

Barn along Crowden Brook.

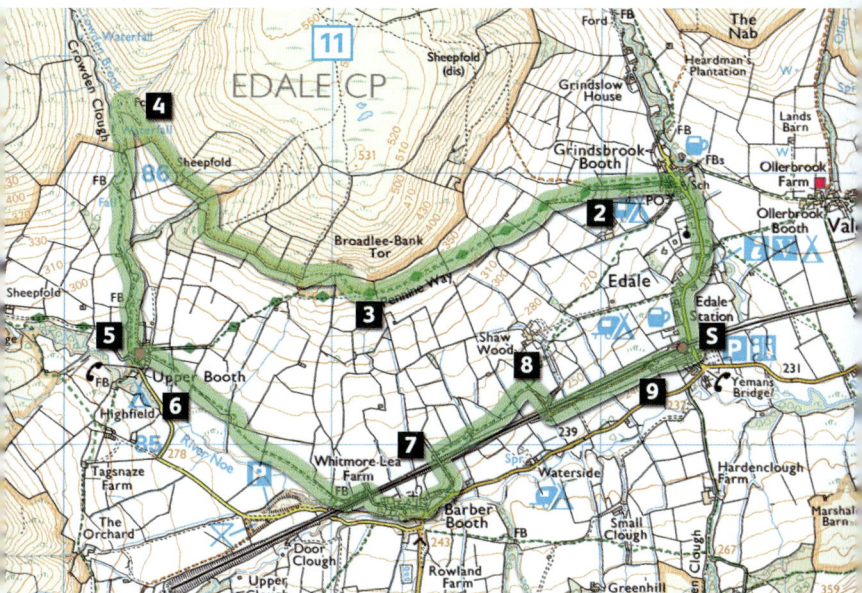

toadstools and other fungi that tend to grow here in autumn. Head over the stile and follow the path past a large barn on the right. Continue for another 200m to reach a short set of steep steps on the left. **Take care** going down the uneven steps, especially after rain. Follow the path through the woodland, which really comes to life with wild flowers during spring. Watch your footing as some sections of the path have partially fallen away.

5 Go through the gate at the end of the woodland path and **turn left** on to the lane to walk over the footbridge and up to Upper Booth. **Turn left** into Upper Booth and walk through the yard past the farm outbuildings. Walk through the wide gate opening (the gate is usually open but there are steps on the left if it's shut) and look out for the signpost on the left marking a public footpath (SK 103 853). **Turn right** to take the public footpath, going through a gate into open pasture.

6 As you walk along the grassy (usually muddy) footpath through the fields, which often have livestock in them, you'll cross two short stone bridges and a wooden bridge. After going through the gate at the wooden bridge, follow the path to the **right** to go through another gate and into another field. After the next gate the footpath is more like a track as it passes through an old camp-site; continue to follow this path and **turn right** to cross over the railway bridge that takes you into the hamlet of Barber Booth. Follow the track through the farm buildings and houses of Barber Booth. Shortly after passing a Methodist chapel on the left, the track meets a T-junction. **Turn left** to walk along the lane for about 80m, then **turn left** to leave the lane and join a track (If you end up on the road then you need to backtrack a few steps).

7 Follow the track and cross the railway bridge. Turn **right** to go through the gate and follow the path. After the next gate, follow the path to the **right** along the edge of the field parallel with the train tracks. Continue on the path through more fields until you reach a signposted concessionary path. **Turn right** towards Edale station.

8 After going through a couple of gates to meet a gravel track, continue on to cross the railway bridge and follow the bend to the left. When the gravel track reaches a field, follow the signposted path towards Edale station across the field, walking parallel to the train tracks which are now on your left.

9 On meeting a short wooden fence at the end of the path, **turn left** to go through a gate into a small woodland, then almost immediately **turn right** to walk towards Edale station car park. If you have time for a brew or an ice cream, the Penny Pot Cafe is conveniently located just past the Edale station entrance.

/ GOOD TO KNOW

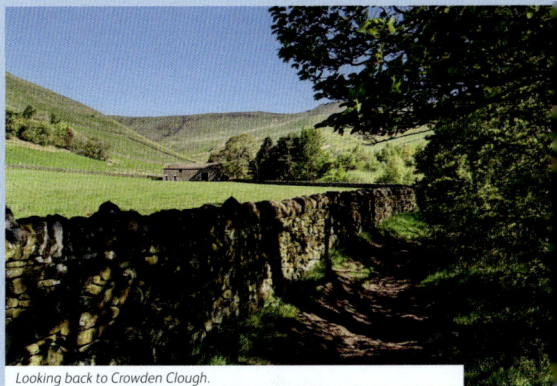
Looking back to Crowden Clough.

PUBLIC TRANSPORT AND ACCESS

Edale sits on the Manchester to Sheffield railway line and is well served by trains daily.

There are pay & display car parks in Edale village and at the station – these can fill up early on fine weather weekends. The Edale Valley is situated just north of the Hope Valley and is easily accessible from the main A6187 road in Hope, or from Mam Nick on the Rushup Edge road west of Mam Tor.

WHEN TO WALK IT

This is a great outing all year round in good weather. It is at its best in the spring because there is more flora to see, but as long as visibility is good it's a lovely walk in any season.

TERRAIN AND NAVIGATION

There are short sections with steep paths, including some uneven steps into the woodland that can be particularly slippery after wet weather. It's advisable to take a map and compass with you as there are a couple of important turning points on this route; these are also a useful precaution in case of low visibility.

FACILITIES AND REFRESHMENTS

There are toilets at the car park and at the Edale visitor centre. The visitor centre has a shop and can provide local information; it's next to the Fieldhead Campsite. The Penny Pot Cafe by Edale station is perfectly placed for pre- or post-walk refreshments. There's also a cafe at Newfold Farm in the middle of the village, as well as a general store. There are also a couple of pubs in the village – the Rambler Inn and the Old Nags Head.

DOGS AND KIDS

Livestock and ground-nesting birds mean Kinder is a dog-on-lead kind of place, particularly between 1 March and 31 July when it is the law under the CRoW Act that dogs must be on short leads. Some of the fields often contain livestock.

This is a kid-friendly walk. Kids (big and little!) might enjoy a paddle in Crowden Brook where the water is usually low near the footbridges.

POINTS OF INTEREST

Built in 1811, Edale Methodist Chapel in Barber Booth is one of the oldest still in regular use.

Edale's booths were founded in the mediaeval period, originally as vaccaries (cattle farms). These settlements were closely linked to the surrounding moorlands which provided summer grazing for livestock and peat for use as a domestic fuel.

6.5km / 4 miles

05 / GRINDSBROOK CLOUGH & GRINDSLOW KNOLL

A medium-difficulty circular walk from Edale up on to the southern edge of Kinder Scout via Grindsbrook Clough, visiting Grindslow Knoll.

/ ESSENTIAL INFO
GRADE ●●○○○
DISTANCE **6.5KM / 4 MILES**
ASCENT **378M**
TIME **2–3 HRS (WALKER)/1–1.5 HRS (RUNNER)**
START/FINISH **EDALE**
START GRID REF **SK 123 853**
START GPS **53.3648, -1.8160**
OS MAP **OL1 THE PEAK DISTRICT: DARK PEAK AREA (1:25,000)**

/ OVERVIEW
At 601 metres on Grindslow Knoll, you'll be standing on one of the highest and finest view-points in the whole of the Peak District. This route starts gently from Edale along a good path with an abundance of streams and cascades on either side, then suddenly climbs quickly and steeply up an easy grade-1 scramble, following the river to the top of the gorge. It can be managed by most walkers with good stamina and suitable footwear. From the top of Grindsbrook Clough, the more prominent peak of Grindslow Knoll is within easy reach, before you descend the steep path back to Edale.

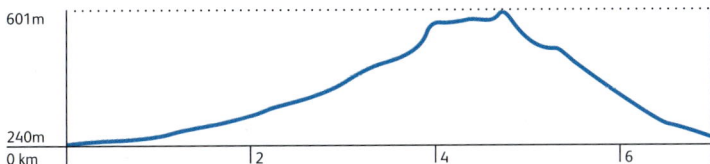

Blooming blossom along Grinds Brook.

Looking down Grindsbrook Clough.

| DIRECTIONS

S From underneath the railway bridge on the road into Edale village, head up into the village. Pass the visitor centre on your right and the church on your left. About 100m after passing the Old Nags Head pub the road turns from tarmac to unsurfaced track. A short distance further on, immediately before white iron gates, a footpath is signed **right** into the woods – take this, cross the river and climb out on the other side, then follow the paved path into open pasture beside the woods.

2 Continue following this low-level path, and go through the gate into a small woodland. On the far side you'll come to an arched bridge over Golden Clough. Listen for the call of the cuckoo in June and buzzards in the summer months. The bridge is a very picturesque spot for photos, looking up to the rocky outcrop of Ringing Roger. Cross the bridge and continue along the path parallel with Grinds Brook for about 1km until the route drops down slightly to meet the river.

> If you've had enough for one day or the weather turns you may wish to retrace your steps at this point because this is where you start to gain altitude, leading to an easy grade 1 scramble.

3 Keep the river to your left as you initially follow the rough path up Grindsbrook Clough, clambering over the rocks. Take your time and don't worry if you need to criss-cross between both sides of the river as you pick your way up to the head of the clough – it's part of the fun! Look for rocks to use as stepping stones over the river but take extra care after heavy rainfall – you don't want soggy feet! En route you'll approach another dramatic gorge towering above you to the right. Have a look but stick with the footpath along the main rocky path up Grinds Brook all the way to the head of the clough.

Grindslow Knoll in summer.

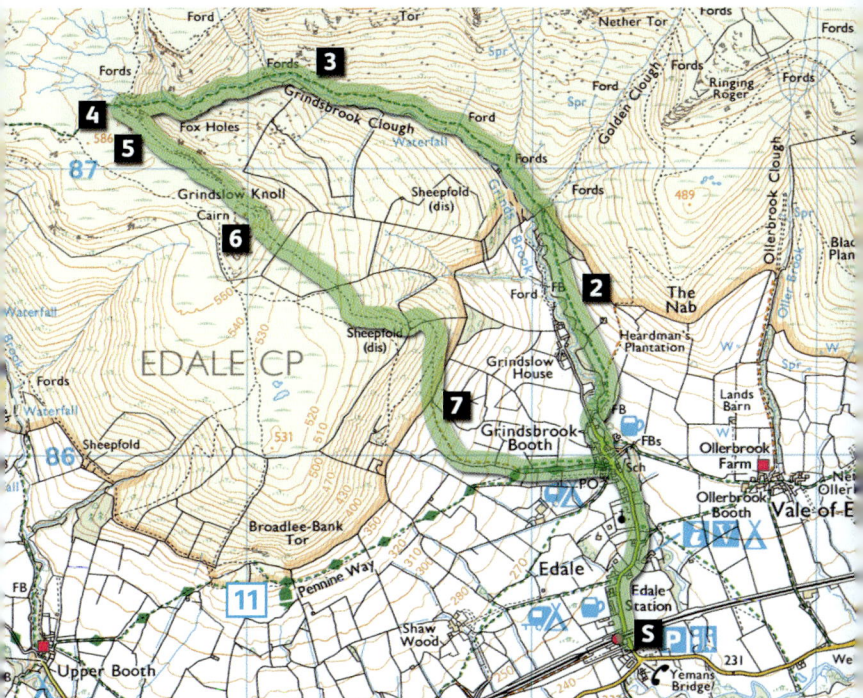

Grindslow Knoll sunset.

4 **Turn left** out of the clough and look for the cairn at the head of Grindsbrook Clough. Here you can take a well-earned rest, and enjoy a brew with a view if you've remembered your flask. Looking back at the way you've come up the clough, on a clear day you can see the Edale Valley and Mam Tor ridge. Look out for kestrels here, often seen hovering the slopes and swooping in for prey.

5 From the cairn, pick up the **south-easterly** path towards Grindslow Knoll. (If visibility is poor, take a bearing of 130° from the cairn.) After 600m the path splits at the base of the knoll; take the **right** incline straight up to the top of the mound where you may have another opportunity for a brew with a view.

6 From the top of the mound on Grindslow Knoll at 601m (sometimes people create a cairn here), follow the same bearing of 130° to pick up the direct path down to Edale. This heads steeply **south-east** for about 1km, eventually reaching a gate into open pasture.

7 Walk down through the pasture until you reach a fingerpost marking the Pennine Way. **Turn left** to follow the tree-lined path back to Edale. Now all you need to do is decide between the cafe or the pub to rest your wobbly legs before retracing your steps to the car park or train station.

GOOD TO KNOW

PUBLIC TRANSPORT AND ACCESS

Edale sits on the Manchester–Sheffield railway line and is well served by trains daily.

There are pay & display car parks in Edale village and at the station; these can fill up early on fine weather weekends. The Edale Valley is situated just north of the Hope Valley and is easily accessible from the main A6187 road in Hope, or from Mam Nick on the Rushup Edge road west of Mam Tor.

WHEN TO WALK IT

This is a great outing all year round, although Grindsbrook Clough is a river so is best avoided after prolonged periods of rain as the water flow spreads and rocks become slippery.

It is best avoided in bad weather which can cling to the cloughs and edges, but those proficient with map and compass will be able to find Grindslow Knoll in low visibility. Heavy rainfall or frozen/icy conditions can make this a dangerous walk.

TERRAIN AND NAVIGATION

There are steep paths and rocky sections on the ascent, descent and along the edge. Grindsbrook Clough is an easy grade-1 scramble. It is advisable to carry a map and compass, and to know how to use them.

FACILITIES AND REFRESHMENTS

There are toilets at the car park and at the Edale visitor centre. The visitor centre also has a shop and can provide local information; it's next to the Fieldhead Campsite. The Penny Pot Cafe by Edale station is perfectly placed for pre- or post-walk refreshments. There's also a cafe at Newfold Farm further into the village, as well as a general store. There are also a couple of pubs in the village – the Rambler Inn and the Old Nags Head.

DOGS AND KIDS

Livestock and ground-nesting birds mean Kinder is a dog-on-lead kind of place, particularly between 1 March and 31 July when it is the law under the CRoW Act that dogs must be on short leads.

This walk is suitable for fit youngsters with appropriate footwear, who are likely to be thrilled by the cascades and giant boulders. There is some easy scrambling involved, but nothing particularly challenging or dangerous. An alternative option is to enjoy just sitting on the riverbanks of Grindsbrook Clough. Note that BBQs are not permitted and bins are not provided.

POINTS OF INTEREST

Edale Church was built in 1885 across the road from two earlier chapels. The stone was quarried from Nether Tor, the rocky outcrop on the southern edge of Kinder that can be seen behind the spire of the church from the village, and towering above while walking along Grinds Brook.

Buzzards can often be seen and heard in the distant trees between Grinds Brook and Grindslow Knoll. They are a bird of prey that soar in high circles over farmland and woodland. The kestrel is also a familiar sight hovering over Grinds Brook, their pointed wings held out when hunting prey.

7km / 4.3 miles

06 / WILDLIFE WALK AROUND KINDER RESERVOIR

A low-level circular walk around Kinder Reservoir from Hayfield, with opportunities to hear the cuckoos in spring and to see geese, grey wagtails and skylarks.

/ ESSENTIAL INFO

GRADE ●●○○

DISTANCE **7KM/4.3 MILES**

ASCENT **240M**

TIME **2.5 HRS (WALKER)/1 HR (RUNNER)**

START/FINISH **HAYFIELD**

START GRID REF **SK 048 869**

START GPS **53.3794, -1.9283**

OS MAP **OL1 THE PEAK DISTRICT: DARK PEAK AREA (1:25,000)**

/ OVERVIEW

Each side of the reservoir offers a unique character and a different view, so it's like doing four walks in one. After a gentle start along the western shore to the foot of William Clough, the route heads east through trees and foxgloves down to the River Kinder. It's worth stopping here for a tea break in good weather to experience the local wildlife and enjoy the unique perspective of looking up to Kinder Downfall in the distance. It then turns south, gaining height into the heather moorland, with superb views of the reservoir, before working round the back of Upper House (a 14th-century (or perhaps older!) farmstead, now a wedding venue), and dropping down to a ford (another tea break spot). It heads west past the reservoir dam before rejoining the Kinder Road into Hayfield.

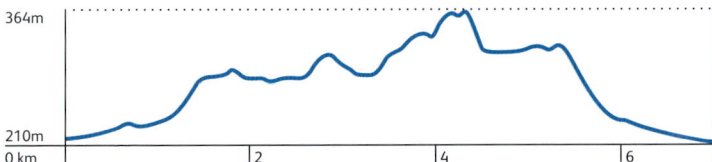

River Kinder flowing into Kinder Reservoir.

View of Kinder Downfall from the path around Kinder Reservoir.

| DIRECTIONS

S Take a look at the plaque commemorating the Kinder Trespass on the quarry side of Bowden Bridge car park before setting off. Then **head north** along Kinder Road to Booth, with the River Kinder running parallel on your right. Note the sign on a gate marking the former site of Kinder station; the railway was built to transport materials and workers to the Kinder Reservoir construction site. After about 700m the lane splits; **take the right fork** to cross the river via Booth Bridge (not the private lane with the green gate), passing an old sheepwash where farmers and shepherds used to do just that – wash their sheep.

2 After 100m the path splits; **follow the fingerpost** to the **left** to go through a gate. Follow the path along the riverbank until meeting a T-junction and **turn left** to cross the river via a footbridge. At the entrance to Kinder Reservoir waterworks (SK 052 880), **bear left** to climb a steep cobbled lane; the reservoir and the edge of Kinder Scout will gradually come into view. After about 250m the path splits; ignore the path on the left and continue, keeping the stone wall on your right. Walk along the edge of Kinder Reservoir to the foot of William Clough at the north end of the reservoir.

3 Cross the footbridge and **follow the path to the right,** parallel with the northern end of the reservoir. After the second gate, continue along the same path down to a narrow stream. Cross the stream and then a stile, following the path down beside a stone wall. At the wire fence, cross the stile and continue on the path to the River Kinder, which is a really great spot for a tea break or lunch, as is the next ford. If you stop here, listen and watch for wildlife while looking up to the impressive Kinder Downfall in the distance to the north-east. You might see grey wagtails and geese by the river.

Kinder Reservoir.

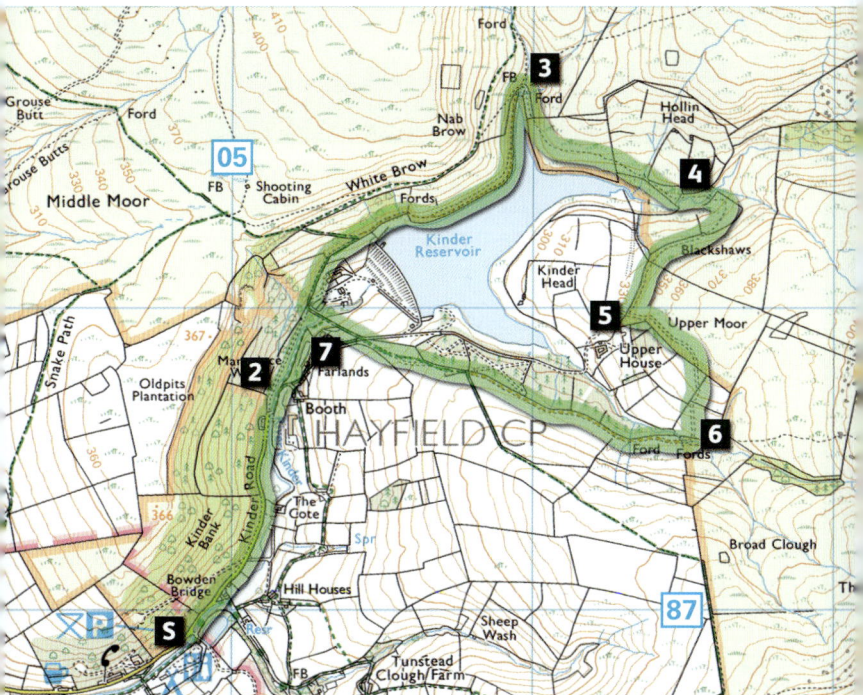

Looking up the River Kinder.

4 Cross the wooden footbridge (SK 065 883). At the crossroads **carry straight on** uphill as the path curves to the right. Listen out for curlew and skylarks as you walk.

5 At the T-junction (SK 063 880) **turn left**, heading towards the corner of a tree plantation with a stone wall around it. Stay on the same track, parallel with the stone wall until a gate. Go through the gate and follow the grassy path downhill. Cross the stile and then find your way over the ford using the stones; take care not to slip. If you saved any lunch or tea, this is the spot you've been waiting for, looking up to The Three Knolls to the south-east while listening to the trickling water.

6 Cross the next stile on the **right** to join a track along the fenced woodland edge for 1km. Continue on the same path downhill (north-west) through open pasture to a gate (SK 054 878). Go through the gate, cross the road and **continue straight** on along a narrow lane that heads steeply downhill to a footbridge.

7 **Turn left** before the footbridge and retrace the outward route to return to the car park.

GOOD TO KNOW

There is a pay & display car park at Bowden Bridge in Hayfield; this can fill up early on fine weekends and during the summer. There Is also roadside parking close by along Kinder Road.

The nearest railway station is in Glossop (8km/ 5 miles from Hayfield). High Peak Bus runs service no. 61 from Glossop to Hayfield bus station which is approximately 1.5km (20 minutes' walk) from the starting point of this walk via Kinder Road. Hulleys runs this service on Sundays.

WHEN TO WALK IT

This is a great outing all year round in fine weather. It is especially pleasant in spring and summer when there is flora and fauna to enjoy, particularly at the northern end of the reservoir.

TERRAIN AND NAVIGATION

This route has good paths and tracks. There is a ford crossing but you can avoid wet feet by stepping on the rocks. Navigation around the reservoir is straightforward but it is advisable to carry a map and compass in case of

Foxgloves growing along the path around Kinder Reservoir.

low visibility. The weather can change quickly and unexpectedly.

FACILITIES AND REFRESHMENTS

There are public toilets available at the start and end of the walk opposite Bowden Bridge car park. It's a small block at the entrance to the Hayfield Campsite.

The Rosie Lee tea room along Kinder Road is well placed for post-walk refreshments. There's also Millie's Tea Room which specialises in chocolate. There are a couple of pubs in the village – the Sportsman Inn and the Pack Horse.

DOGS AND KIDS

Livestock and ground-nesting birds mean Kinder is a dog-on-lead kind of

place, particularly between 1 March and 31 July when it is the law under the CRoW Act that dogs must be on short leads.

This is a really nice route to walk with family and can be a relaxing day out with a picnic. Kids might enjoy a paddle in the River Kinder or at the fords.

POINTS OF INTEREST

Hayfield village was historically a staging post on the trading packhorse route across the Pennines from Cheshire to Yorkshire.

Kinder Reservoir was constructed between 1903 and 1911 to supply water to the Stockport area. It opened in 1912.

Upper House was passed for generations through the Kinder family; its earliest records date back to 1378.

9.5km / 5.9 miles

07 / SUNSET WALK ON RUSHUP EDGE

A circular route from Edale up to Rushup Edge, walking along the ridge and visiting its highest point at Lord's Seat.

/ ESSENTIAL INFO

GRADE ●●○○○
DISTANCE **9.5KM/5.9 MILES**
ASCENT **365M**
TIME **3.5 HRS (WALKER)/1 HR 45 MINS (RUNNER)**
START/FINISH **EDALE**
START GRID REF **SK 123 853**
START GPS **53.3648, -1.8160**
OS MAP **OL1 THE PEAK DISTRICT: DARK PEAK AREA (1:25,000)**

/ OVERVIEW

It's a steep climb from Edale Valley up to Rushup Edge, but once you're on the ridge it feels well worth it for the views – especially when you time it to watch the sun go down. Set off a good 90 minutes before sunset (unless you're running) and don't forget your head torch, map and compass – maybe sunglasses too! This route gains height quickly out of Edale up to Mam Nick via Harden Clough, then takes the most direct route up to Rushup Edge and heads west along the ridge, visiting Lord's Seat (an ancient bowl barrow). At the end of the ridge it turns right down the Chapel Gate track, before passing through open pasture in the valley back to Edale.

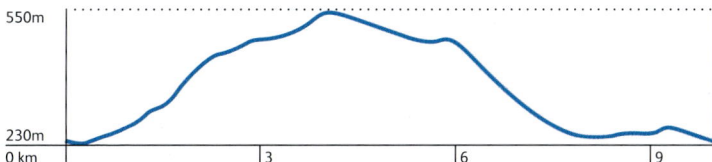

View to Kinder Scout from Harden Clough.

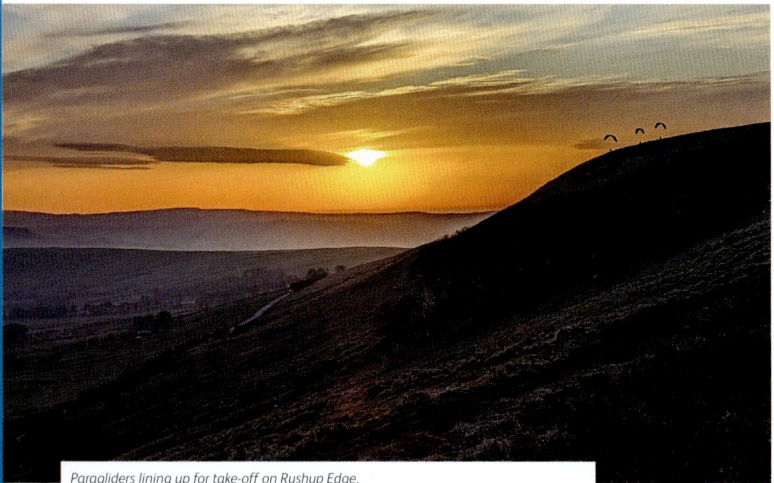

Paragliders lining up for take-off on Rushup Edge.

⎮ DIRECTIONS

S From underneath the railway bridge on the road into Edale village, head south to Edale Road. **Turn right** at the T-junction and walk along the road for about 50m until you reach a lane on the left. **Take this** for 400m to Hardenclough Farm where you can buy snacks (honesty box). Walk past the farm and continue up the lane, parallel with a stream on the left. After 250m there's a junction. Stick with the lane as it bends to the left (east) and crosses the stream. Continue to a gate just before Greenlands house.

2 Go through the gate and **turn right** to go through a second gate. Follow this steep but steady path up for 900m to a gate on to a road lay-by. Carefully cross the road and walk up it until a stile (SK 124 834) to the **right**. Cross the stile and take the steep uphill path to Rushup Edge ridge.

3 Walk along Rushup Edge for 1.2km to Lord's Seat. There may be paragliders whizzing by overhead as this is a popular place for the sport in certain conditions. Lord's Seat is a bowl barrow, likely to be late Neolithic to early Bronze Age and containing one or more burials. It used to be fenced off but at the time of writing only the wooden fence posts remain, along with a National Trust sign asking people not to walk on the mound to avoid further erosion. Although it may be tempting to use it as a viewing platform, please refrain as there are plenty of excellent viewpoints around the mound's perimeter. Looking back towards Mam Tor ridge as the sun sets can be a spectacular sight!

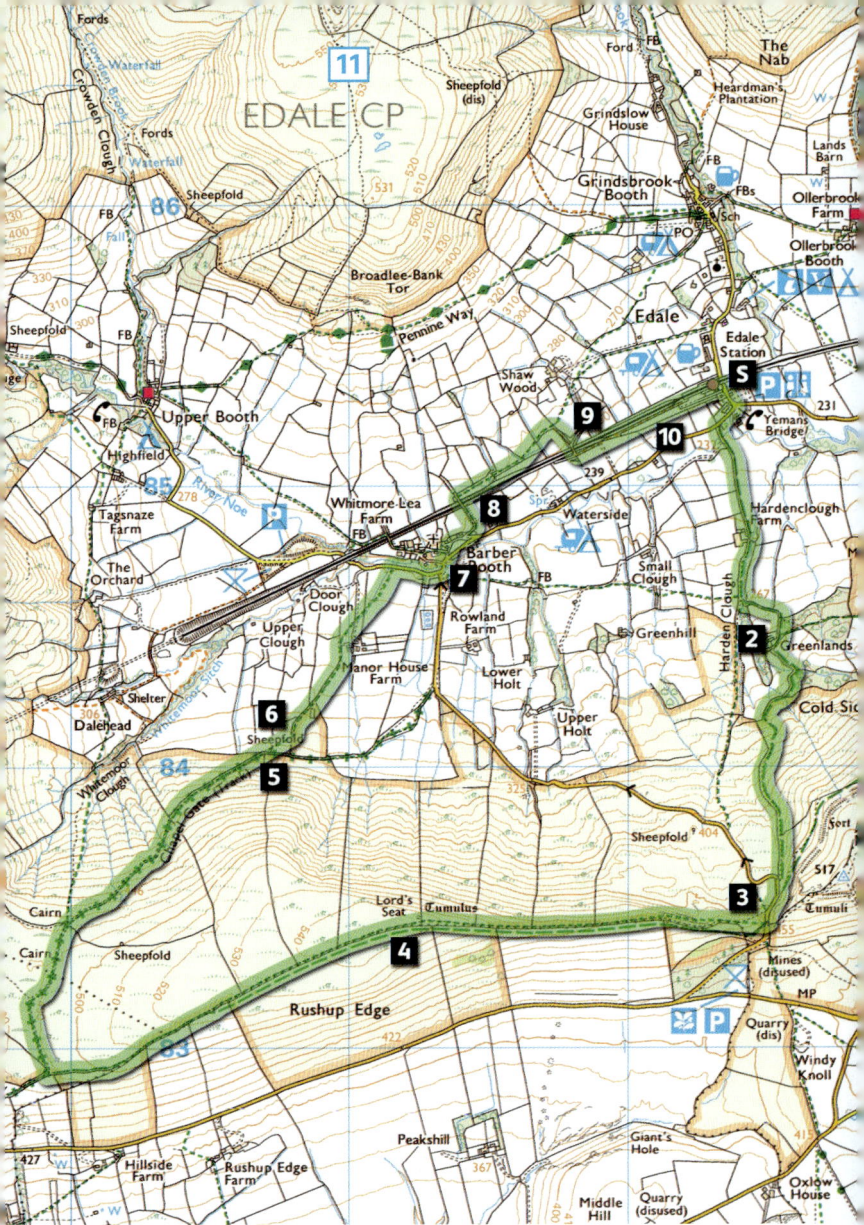

4 Continue along the ridge path for 1.4km to a junction marked by a signpost. **Turn right** to join Chapel Gate track (north) and follow this for 500m (ignoring the flagstone path that heads west after the first 250m). At the next junction (SK 099 834) stick with the wide track that now heads north-east for 1km.

5 At the large metal gate (SK 106 840) go through the wooden side gate. Immediately on the **left** is another wooden gate with a public footpath arrow on it. **Take this** to leave the track and **head north-east** (bearing of 63°) through open pasture towards a small wooden gate. Go through the gate and continue in the same direction for about 50m to an old stone guidepost (SK 107 841).

6 Immediately after the stone guidepost, **turn left** to head north for 50m. At the corner of the stone wall (SK 108 841) next to another stone guidepost, **head north-east on a bearing of 39°** for about 50m to a gate. **Turn left** after going through the gate to follow a path past Manor House Farm. This section is better signposted, passing several stiles and gates with public footpath arrows on them. The final stile brings you to a lane parallel with the River Noe (SK 111 847). **Turn right** on to the lane and follow this for 150m to the junction with Edale Road.

7 **Turn left** at the junction, and then **almost immediately left again** at the second lane (SK 113 847) that leads into the hamlet of Barber Booth. Continue along the lane as it bends right past some houses. After the last house, take the **track on the left** (if you end up on the road again you've walked too far and need to retrace a few steps back to take the signposted track).

8 After about 100m along the track, cross the railway bridge and then almost immediately **turn right** through a gate and follow the path through a field. After the next gate, follow the grassy path to the right along the edge of the field parallel with the train tracks. Continue on the path through more fields until you reach a signposted concessionary path. **Take the right** towards Edale station.

9 After going through a couple of gates to meet a gravel track, head on to cross the railway bridge and follow the bend to the left. When the gravel track meets a field, follow the signposted path towards Edale station across the field, walking parallel to the train tracks which are now on your left.

10 At a short wooden fence at the end of the path, **turn left** to go through a gate into a small woodland, then almost immediately **turn right** towards Edale Station and car park. To get to the main car park, **turn right** after passing the Penny Pot Cafe and then cross the road through a cutting into the car park.

/ GOOD TO KNOW

Edale sits on the Manchester–Sheffield railway line and is well served by trains daily.

There are pay & display car parks in Edale village and at the station; these can fill up early on fine weekends. The Edale Valley is situated just north of the Hope Valley and is easily accessible from the main A6187 road in Hope, or from Mam Nick on the Rushup Edge road west of Mam Tor.

WHEN TO WALK IT

This is a great outing all year round. It is best avoided after prolonged periods of rain or in bad weather which can hang around on the ridge. It is particularly enjoyable around sunset, especially when paragliders are up there.

TERRAIN AND NAVIGATION

There are steep paths on the ascent and descent, and uneven ground with loose stones and rocks underfoot. Navigation is quite straightforward but it is advisable to carry a map and compass, and to know how to use them. Remember your headtorch!

Winter sunset along Rushup Edge.

FACILITIES AND REFRESHMENTS

There are toilets at the car park and at the Edale visitor centre. The visitor centre also has a shop and can provide local information; it's next to Fieldhead Campsite. Depending on the time of year, these will be most likely be closed following a sunset walk. The Penny Pot Cafe by Edale station is perfectly placed for pre- or post-walk refreshments during the daytime. There's also a cafe and bistro at Newfold Farm further into the village, as well as a general store. There are also a couple of pubs in the village – the Rambler Inn and the Old Nags Head.

DOGS AND KIDS

Livestock and ground-nesting birds mean Kinder is a dog-on-lead kind of place, particularly between 1 March and 31 July when it is the law under the CRoW Act that dogs must be on short leads.

This walk is suitable for kids as long as they can handle the steep ascent at the start, as the route then flattens out nicely along the ridge. They might enjoy watching paragliders on Rushup Edge if the weather is suitable.

POINTS OF INTEREST

The summit of Mam Tor is the largest of a small group of hillforts in the Peak District dating from the Bronze Age.

There is a well-preserved bowl barrow at Lord's Seat, likely to be late Neolithic to early Bronze Age and containing one or more burials.

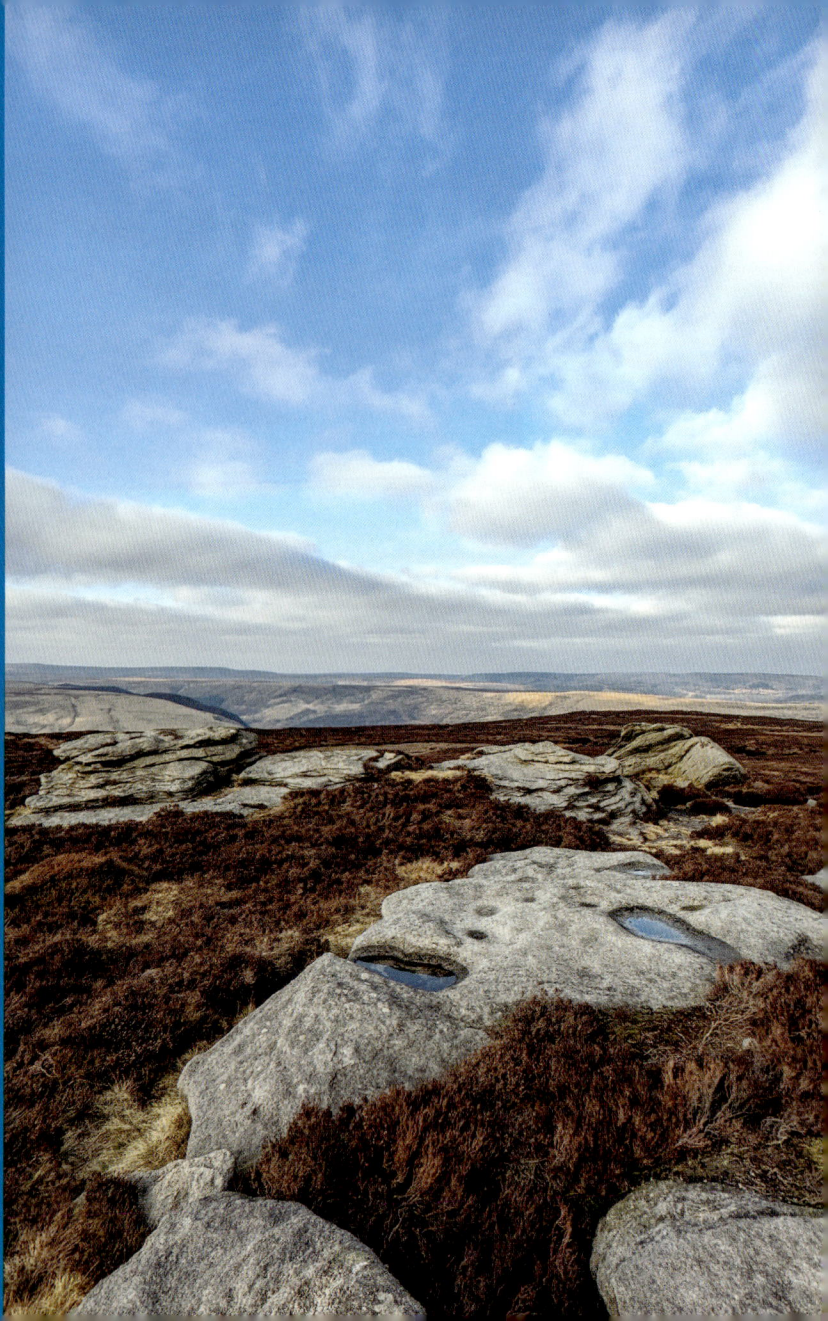

12km / 7.5 miles

08 / THE LONELY TRIG POINT

A high-level circular walk from Edale up on to the Kinder plateau via Ringing Roger, visiting Madwoman's Stones and the Lonely Trig Point.

/ ESSENTIAL INFO

GRADE ● ● ○ ○
DISTANCE **12 KM/7.5 MILES**
ASCENT **400M**
TIME **4 HRS (WALKER)/2.5 HRS (RUNNER)**
START/FINISH **EDALE**
START GRID REF **SK 123 853**
START GPS **53.3648, -1.8160**
OS MAP **OL1 THE PEAK DISTRICT: DARK PEAK AREA (1:25,000)**

/ OVERVIEW

It's approximately 300 hard-won metres from the valley to the plateau top, and once there it's well worth going for a good exploration. This route climbs quickly and steeply out of Edale on to The Nab and the rocky crest of Ringing Roger (also known as 'Ringing Rock'), then hangs a right and heads east along the edge of the plateau before following a small stream into the heart of the Kinder plateau, visiting Madwoman's Stones and the Lonely Trig Point on Edale Moor. Now it's time to really put your waterproof boots to the test through the peaty groughs! From here, it returns to the rim of the plateau and works west along the edge before descending the somewhat tiring Grinds Brook back to Edale.

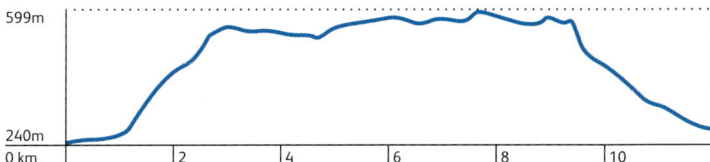

Madwoman's Stones.

| DIRECTIONS

S From underneath the railway bridge on the road into Edale village, head up into the village. Pass the visitor centre on your right and the church on your left. About 100m after the Old Nags Head pub the road changes from tarmac to unsurfaced track. A short distance further on, immediately before white iron gates, a footpath is signed **right** into the woods – **take this**, cross the river via the footbridge, and follow the paved path into open pasture alongside the woods.

2 After 100m, just after passing a small stone barn on the left, the path splits. Take the permissive footpath to the **right** that trends uphill to a gate and a small tree plantation. Go through the gate, take a breather to look at the view of Edale below, then follow the steps and path that zigzags left and right up on to The Nab which has a small rocky crest with a wonderful view of Edale and the Mam Tor ridge. From here, cut back **sharp left** up the rough steps then follow the path north towards the Kinder plateau. The rocky outcrop of Ringing Roger will appear up ahead. Ignoring the first path to the right, take the **right fork** where the path splits, climbing the steps towards Ringing Roger. When you reach the rocky climb to your right (SK 124 871) follow the line of most resistance almost directly up the nose (the path was recently repaired), passing several interesting boulders until eventually you reach the edge path which runs along the plateau rim.

3 Head **north-east** along the good path, parallel with the plateau edge to the right. You will soon cross a series of small fords (Oller Brook). Keep going for another 1.3km along the edge path to the next large ford (SK 138 878).

> If visibility is poor, you may wish to retrace your steps at this point because in poor weather the centre of the plateau is a really easy place to get lost.

4 **Turn left** and follow the course of the stream for 200m, clambering over rocks at first and heading into the moor proper, picking up a vague path to the right of the stream. There's heather, cottongrass, peat and sphagnum in abundance thanks to the work of Moors For The Future. You'll come to a small trod on the right (SK 136 877), which is no more than a sheep track; follow this for 300m north to Madwoman's Stones. If visibility is good, you'll soon see the boulders coming into view on the horizon. Lunch here? In the near distance you'll see the landslip of Alport Castles to the north and Derwent Edge to the east.

Almost directly west is the lonely trig (590m above sea level); you'll be able to see it if you followed the advice to do this walk in good weather! You can follow

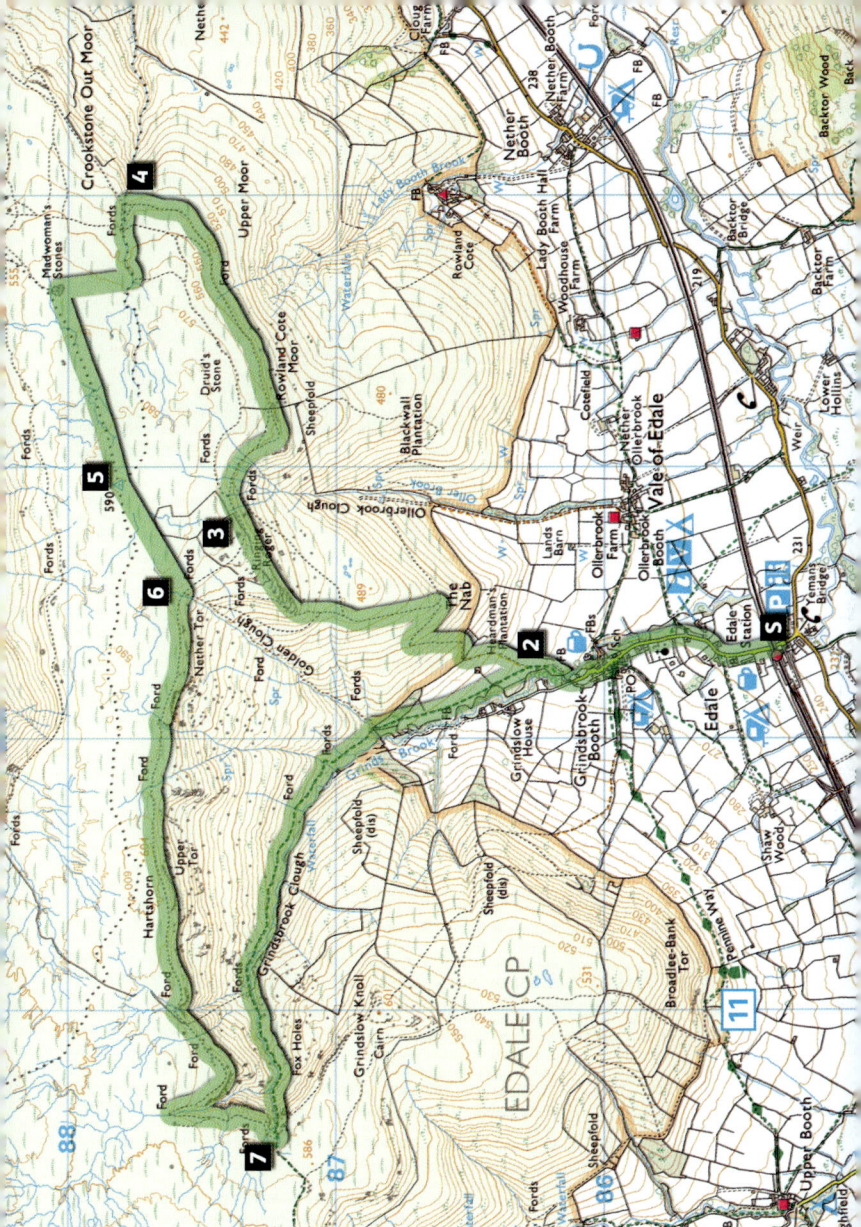

The lonely trig point on Edale Moor.

a vague path to the trig point from Madwoman's Stones, or follow a bearing of 250° for about 700m. If you've saved your lunch, the trig is a great location for a rest with fine views. On the way there you may notice gully blockages and dams. This is part of a peat bog restoration project (see opposite).

5 From the trig point, an even vaguer path heads south-west across a couple of quintessential hags and groughs before picking up the path at the edge of the plateau. There will be some peat bog dodging involved so watch your footing. Ideally you'll meet the edge path at the head of Golden Clough (SK 125 875).

> From here, you can turn left (east) back to Ringing Roger and descend the path used in ascent and return to Edale using the outward route.

6 **Turn right** (west) and follow the path along the edge of the plateau for 2.5km to the head of Grinds Brook – the clough of the same name is always visible below you to the left. Along the way you'll pass several small fords and a deep gorge that feeds into Grinds Brook. **Cross the large ford** (SK 106 875), which may or may not be dry, and **turn sharp left** to continue along the high path along the edge to the head of Grinds Brook.

7 **Turn left** off the edge and descend the path beside the water course. The path is good and increasingly easy to follow, though there's a bit of a steep clamber over rocks at first and it can be tiring at the end of the day. Continue on the footpath beside Grinds Brook all the way down the valley towards Edale, picking up and reversing the outward route once you are back at the stone barn below The Nab. Once back in the village you have various options for pubs and cafes.

| GOOD TO KNOW

Edale sits on the Manchester–Sheffield railway line and is well served by trains daily.

There are pay & display car parks in Edale village and at the station; these can fill up early on fine weekends.

WHEN TO WALK IT

This is a great outing all year round, although as the plateau is a raised blanket bog it is best avoided after prolonged periods of rain.

It is best avoided in bad weather which can hang around on the plateau. The reduced (and at times zero) visibility and lack of landmarks make this a dull and possibly dangerous walk in such conditions, even for those proficient with map and compass.

TERRAIN AND NAVIGATION

There are steep paths and rocky sections on the ascent, descent and along the edge, and the moorland section is exposed with faint paths/trods. It is advisable to carry a map and compass, and to know how to use them.

There are peat bogs on this route so it's worth putting on your waterproof boots, especially after a spell of wet weather. Walking poles and gaiters can also come in handy.

FACILITIES AND REFRESHMENTS

There are toilets at the car park and at the Edale visitor centre. The visitor centre also has a shop and can provide local information. The Penny Pot Cafe by Edale station is perfectly placed for pre- or post-walk refreshments. There's also a cafe at Newfold Farm, as well as a general store. There are a couple of pubs in the village – the Rambler Inn and the Old Nags Head.

DOGS AND KIDS

Livestock and ground-nesting birds mean Kinder is a dog-on-lead kind of place, particularly between 1 March and 31 July when it is the law under the CRoW Act that dogs must be on short leads.

This walk is eminently escapable at most points by simply turning back, so it is a good choice for fit and adventurous youngsters. Another option is to miss out the loop round Madwoman's Stones and the trig, and simply head west along the edge path to Grinds Brook after climbing Ringing Roger.

POINTS OF INTEREST

The Moors For The Future Partnership aims to reverse historic damage to the moorland plants on Kinder Scout (and other areas of the Peak District and South Pennine moors), in which air pollution and wildfire killed off huge areas of vegetation. Their work includes re-wetting the moors by planting sphagnum moss and blocking erosion gullies with small dams to slow the flow of the water and raise the water table. These dams are made of heather bales, peat, plastic, stone and timber.

Sphagnum moss is a moorland plant that is able to absorb up to 20 times its own weight in water. By storing water it prevents the decay of dead plant material and eventually forms peat. It significantly slows down the water run-off from the hills after rainfall, and therefore reduces flood risk.

The summit plateau is a National Nature Reserve, and Kinder is managed by the National Trust. Access to some areas of the moor is restricted at certain times of year due to walk-up grouse shooting so it's best to check ahead of your visit.

12km / 7.5 miles

09 / HAYFIELD TO KINDER DOWNFALL & KINDER LOW

A high-level circular walk from Hayfield up on to the Kinder plateau via the reservoir, visiting the Downfall and Kinder Low trig.

/ ESSENTIAL INFO

GRADE ●●○○

DISTANCE **12 KM/7.5 MILES**

ASCENT **550M**

TIME **4–5 HRS (WALKER)/2.5 HRS (RUNNER)**

START/FINISH **HAYFIELD**

START GRID REF **SK 048 869**

START GPS **53.3794, -1.9283**

OS MAP **OL1 THE PEAK DISTRICT: DARK PEAK AREA (1:25,000)**

/ OVERVIEW

This walk is steeped in history from its beginning at the start point of the 1932 mass trespass. The route begins fairly gently beside the river and Kinder Reservoir, before climbing steeply up to the Kinder plateau – you may need to pause for a few breathers. In good weather the ascent is worth it for the views at the top – promise! It then hangs a right and heads east along the edge of the plateau to the Downfall (which might be an 'upfall' if you've picked a particularly windy day). From here, it turns south to the trig pillar at Kinder Low and then follows a good path steeply down to Kinderlow End before returning to Hayfield via open pasture.

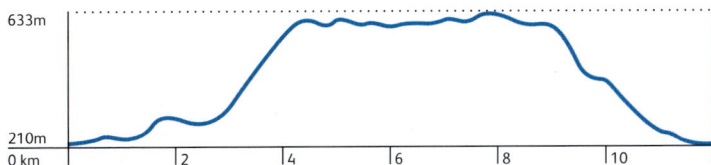

View of Kinder Reservoir from the plateau edge.

Looking back to Kinderlow End.

| DIRECTIONS

S Take a look at the commemorative plaque on the quarry side of Bowden Bridge car park before setting off. Then **head north** along Kinder Road to Booth, with the River Kinder running parallel on your right. Note the sign on a gate marking the former site of Kinder station, built to transport materials and workers to the Kinder Reservoir construction site. After about 700m where the lane splits, **take the right** to cross the river over Booth Bridge (not the private lane with the green gate to Kinder Reservoir), passing an old sheepwash where farmers and shepherds used to wash their sheep.

2 After 100m the lane splits; **follow the fingerpost** to the **left** to go through a gate. Follow the path along the riverbank until meeting a T-junction and **turn left** to cross the river via a footbridge. At the entrance to Kinder Reservoir waterworks (SK 052 880), **bear left** to climb a steep cobbled lane, with the reservoir and the edge of Kinder Scout gradually coming into view. After about 250m the path splits; **ignore** the path that bends left uphill and **continue straight on**, keeping the stone wall on your right. Walk along the edge of Kinder Reservoir to the foot of William Clough at the north end of the reservoir.

> If visibility is poor, you may wish to turn back and retrace your steps at this point because in poor weather the edge of the plateau is exposed to the elements and becomes a challenge for navigation.

Kinder Scout National Nature Reserve
Kinder Downfall
Kinder Gates
Edale Head
Pym Chair
The Cloughs
Jacob's Ladder (Path)
Noe Stool
Kinder Low
Edale Rocks
Swine's Back
Sheepfold
Pennine Way
Cluther Rocks
Mermaid's Pool
Sandy Heys
The Three Knolls
Kinderlow Cavern
Kinderlow End
Broad Clough
Upper Moor
Blackshaws
Hollin Head
Upper House
Kinder Head
Kinder Reservoir
HAYFIELD
Sheep Wash
Tunstead Clough Farm
The Ashes
Harry Moor
Stony Ford
William Clough
Nab Brow
White Brow
Leygatehead Moor
Shooting Cabin
Grouse Butts
The Knott
Middle Moor
Farlands
Booth
The Gote
Hill Houses
Kinder Road
Kinder Bank
Bowden Bridge
Oldpits Plantation
Snake Path
Stones House
Elle Bank
Quarry (dis)
Stubbs Farm
Highgate Head
05
89
S
2
3
4
5
6
7
8

3 Cross the footbridge and take the few steps on the left to join a steep moorland trod heading north-east up to Kinder Scout plateau. If in doubt, **walk on a bearing of 62°** from the footbridge. After about 1.25km of slogging uphill, the trod meets a path along the edge. **Turn right** here to follow the path south-east as it winds between rocks and boulders all the way to the head of Kinder Downfall. If visibility is good there are fantastic views of Kinder Reservoir, Mount Famine and South Head.

4 Cross the river at the head of Kinder Downfall (SK 083 889), which famously becomes an 'upfall' in very strong winds. **Turn sharp right** to continue along the edge path in a southerly direction (remember to look back towards the gorge to see the Downfall), picking your way between the rocks and making sure that you don't lose too much elevation.

5 1km from the Downfall, cross the ford at Red Brook (SK 080 880) and stay on the edge path for 600m. If there is confusion about paths, **walk on a bearing of 204°** until the path splits at a large cairn (SK 078 873). **Take the left fork** that initially trends gently uphill. It's about 400m to the trig pillar from the cairn. In good visibility, Kinder Low trig pillar will come into view elevated on a large boulder and surrounded by other large boulders. Walk towards this and take in the views of Pym Chair and the Pagoda to the east, or of Manchester and beyond to the west.

6 The paths can be a bit confusing from the Kinder Low trig pillar, so it's best to **walk on a bearing of 240°** for 50m to a large cairn and **turn left** to join a path that heads south-west for 350m. At the junction of flagstone paths **keep right** to stay on the same path, heading west towards a Bronze Age burial mound (SK 073 866). Continue past the mound for 400m, then head down the path that steeply descends good steps towards a gate.

7 Take the gate to your **left**, then follow the moorland path for 100m before taking the next gate on the **right** through a stone wall (SK 064 866). There is a National Trust signpost next to it marking Kinderlow End. Head west through a large gap in a stone wall and continue through open pasture for about 1km towards Tunstead Clough Farm, crossing several stiles along the way.

8 **Turn right** after the farmhouse to follow the lane as it zigzags downhill towards Hayfield. At the crossroads head **straight on**. Before you know it you'll be back at the car park trying to decide between the tea rooms or one of the pubs.

GOOD TO KNOW

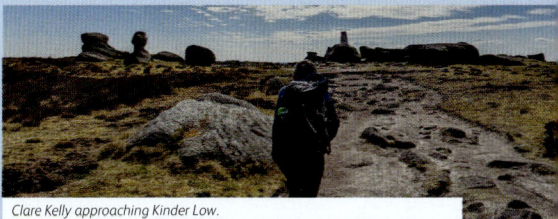
Clare Kelly approaching Kinder Low.

PUBLIC TRANSPORT AND ACCESS

There is a pay & display car park at Bowden Bridge in Hayfield; this can fill up early on fine weather weekends and during the summer. There is also roadside parking along Kinder Road nearby.

The nearest railway station is in Glossop (8km/ 5 miles from Hayfield). High Peak Bus runs service no. 61 from Glossop to Hayfield bus station which is approximately 1.6km along Kinder Road from the starting point of this walk, which adds about 20 minutes each way. Hulleys runs this service on Sundays.

WHEN TO WALK IT

This is a great outing all year round, although as the plateau is a raised blanket bog it is best avoided after prolonged periods of rain.

It is also best avoided in bad weather which can hang around on the plateau. The reduced (and at times zero) visibility and lack of landmarks make this a dull and possibly dangerous walk in such conditions.

TERRAIN AND NAVIGATION

There are steep paths on the ascent and descent and it's rocky with uneven ground along the edge of the plateau. Map and compass skills are necessary, especially in low visibility.

FACILITIES AND REFRESHMENTS

There is a small public toilet block at the start and end of the walk at the entrance to Hayfield Campsite opposite Bowden Bridge car park.

The Rosie Lee tea room along Kinder Road is well placed for post-walk refreshments. There's also Millie's Tea Room which specialises in chocolate. There are a couple of pubs in the village – the Sportsman Inn and the Pack Horse.

DOGS AND KIDS

Livestock and ground-nesting birds mean Kinder is a dog-on-lead kind of place, particularly between 1 March and 31 July when it is the law under the CRoW Act that dogs must be on short leads.

There is nothing especially dangerous about this walk and it is eminently escapable at most points by simply turning back, so it can be a good – and fun – choice for fit and adventurous youngsters. There is the alternative option of walking around Kinder Reservoir if legs are too tired for the steep climb up to the plateau, or if the weather turns. See page 29.

POINTS OF INTEREST

Bowden Bridge was the rallying point for the 1932 mass trespass on Kinder Scout, an iconic event in the campaign for access to the countryside.

Kinderlow bowl barrow is a well-preserved example of a Bronze Age burial mound which appears to have escaped excavation in the 19th century and is believed to contain rare intact archae-ological remains. It is a scheduled monument.

The arched packhorse bridge over the River Kinder (SK 050 870) is thought to have been built in the 18th century, situated on the old packhorse route between Edale and Holmfirth.

THE NATIONAL TRUST

HIGH PEAK ESTATE

JACOBS LADDER

13km / 8.1 miles

10 / JACOB'S LADDER & THE WOOLPACKS

A high-level circular walk from Edale up on to the Kinder plateau via Jacob's Ladder and the Woolpacks, visiting Edale Cross.

/ ESSENTIAL INFO

GRADE ●●○○○
DISTANCE **13KM/8.1 MILES**
ASCENT **550M**
TIME **4.5 HRS (WALKER)/2.5 HRS (RUNNER)**
START/FINISH **EDALE**
START GRID REF **SK 123 853**
START GPS **53.3648, -1.8160**
OS MAP **OL1 THE PEAK DISTRICT: DARK PEAK AREA (1:25,000)**

/ OVERVIEW

This walk is full of intriguing rock formations, relics of packhorse routes and awe-inspiring views. It will be especially appealing to landscape photographers, artists and rock clamberers. The route begins fairly gently along the start of the Pennine Way, then climbs steeply up Jacob's Ladder and on to Edale Cross (ancient boundary marker) and the rocky outcrop of Swine's Back. From here, it drops down to the giant boulders of Noe Stool, then the Pagoda, and then heads through the Woolpacks (an impressive sprawl of weathered boulders that resemble mythical creatures). After the boulder maze it continues to Crowden Tower, over Crowden Brook and along the rim of the plateau, then climbs up Grindslow Knoll before descending steeply back to Edale (and the pub!).

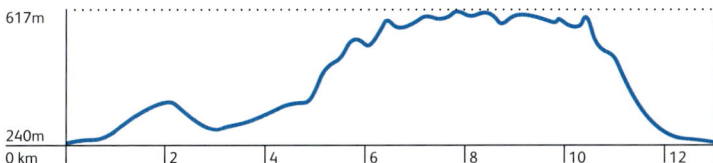

Jacob's Ladder.

Fingerpost in Grindsbrook Booth.

| DIRECTIONS

S From underneath the railway bridge on the road into Edale village, head up into the village. Pass the visitor centre on your right and the church on your left. A short distance further on, immediately before reaching the Old Nags Head, the Pennine Way is signed **left** on a fingerpost – **take this** narrow tree-lined footpath alongside a stream.

2 After 300m the path splits; **take the left fork** through the gate, following the signposted Pennine Way. Keep going for 900m through open pasture and listen out for the call of the curlew if you're walking this route in the spring or summer. There's a good bench for a sit along the way.

3 After going through a gate the path briefly ascends more steeply. **Keep straight on**, walking towards a drystone wall with a gate in the middle. Go through the gate and descend the path that winds between two hillocks. After another gate you will pass a ruined farm building on your left. Continue along the footpath towards the farm and houses at Upper Booth.

4 At the end of the footpath, go through the gate that brings you to a T-junction. **Turn left** along the lane and walk through Upper Booth hamlet and farmyard. **Turn right** on to the road and follow it to Lee Farm where there are a few houses and farm outbuildings (ignore the sign on the metal gate that says *Residents only beyond this point* as this only applies to vehicles, not walkers). Pass the houses at Lee Farm and before going through the gate ahead, note the National Trust barn on the left which has a public information display and provides a really good shelter from the rain or wind if you need a tea break.

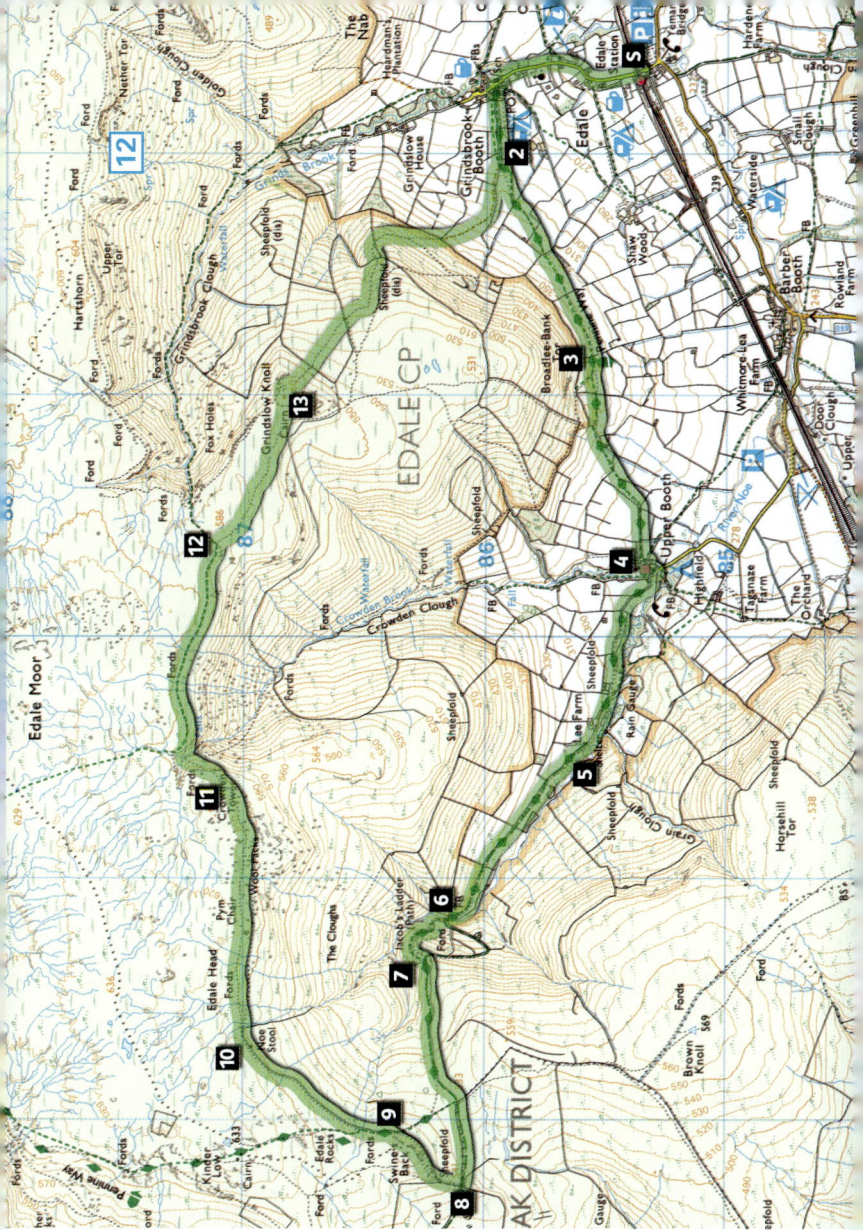

Evening light on the Woolpacks.

5 Go through the gate and continue along the track until you reach a narrow stone bridge over the River Noe. Cross the bridge and if the sun is shining consider sitting on the riverbank for tea and snacks – you've got a steep climb up Jacob's Ladder coming up next! While you sit and listen to the cascades, imagine lines of packhorses and their drivers or 'jaggers' passing through here along the historical trade route between Edale and Hayfield on the way to Stockport.

6 From the National Trust sign for *Jacob's Ladder*, ascend the steep staircase on the **right**, which is named after Jacob Marshall, who created the original shortcut up the bank in the 18th century. Jacob would walk up this while his packhorses were sent up the gentler winding track – now a bridleway busy with mountain bikes. It's quite a slog up the staircase so take your time. Eventually you'll reach a large stone cairn where you can have a rest and enjoy the reward of the climb – a great view!

> If the weather is poor, you may wish to turn back and retrace your steps at this point because the Kinder plateau is exposed to the elements and can be tricky to navigate.

Noe Stool.

7 From the cairn, follow the bridleway ascending west for about 500m. At the junction, turn **left** along a narrow footpath (not the flagstone path). Go through the gate and continue **west** for 350m along a wide bridleway. Go through a gap in a stone wall; immediately to your right is a small stone enclosure containing the Edale Cross, a mediaeval boundary marker or guidestone.

8 Retrace your steps back through the gap in the stone wall; almost immediately to your **left** is a gate and an uphill footpath. **Take this**, initially following the line of the stone wall uphill. After passing the stone ruins on your right (SK 077 862), **fork right** to follow a faint path up the crest of Swine's Back hill, passing a few large boulders and leading to a rocky outcrop. Enjoy this unique perspective of Kinder Scout and beyond!

9 With the rocky outcrop to your right, descend the short, steep moorland path to join the flagstone path below. Follow this for about 100m, passing three cairns. At the larger third cairn, take the rough and rocky path on the **right** for about 550m until you reach Noe Stool – an impressive anvil-shaped boulder overlooking the River Noe below. Lunch here if you have any left.

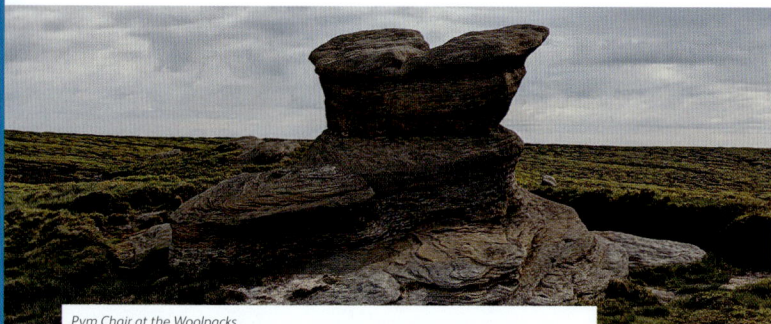

Pym Chair at the Woolpacks.

10 Walking past Noe Stool, **head east** along the path that drops down slightly to a large cairn. Follow the flagstones up towards a giant boulder formation called the Pagoda – another excellent viewpoint and a great place to have a clamber about (the OS map only mentions Pym Chair, a smaller but still noticeable boulder behind the Pagoda). **Keep heading east** towards the Woolpacks – a sprawling cluster of weathered boulders named for their resemblance to the bales of wool carried by packhorses. There are pathless, boggy sections through the maze of boulders, which can get confusing. It may be worth **walking on a bearing of 75°** from the Pagoda to Crowden Tower to keep on track for 550m. Crowden Tower is an outcrop of boulders overlooking Crowden Brook – a remarkable view!

11 Pick up the path just behind the boulders of Crowden Tower to drop down steeply to the stream crossing at the head of Crowden Brook (SK 094 872). Enjoy the view here of Mam Tor framed by Crowden Brook's ravine. After crossing the shallow stream, cut up the steep bank to rejoin the easterly path along the edge for about 750m.

12 **Turn right** at the junction (SK 103 871) to join a flagstone path that leads to the top of Grindslow Knoll. Where the flagstones end, walk up the steep grassy path to the highest point at the top of the knoll where there are the remains of a cairn. How far can you see from here? Take a final look before you start walking back down to Edale.

13 From the summit cairn of Grindslow Knoll, walk about 50m on a compass bearing of **130°** to pick up the direct path to Edale. This heads steeply south-east for about 1km, eventually reaching a gate into open pasture. Take your time as there are a lot of loose rocks. Walk down through the pasture until you reach a fingerpost marking the Pennine Way. **Turn left** to follow the tree-lined path back to Edale.

GOOD TO KNOW

Edale sits on the Manchester–Sheffield railway line and is well served by trains daily.

There are pay & display car parks in Edale village and at the station; these can fill up early on sunny weekends. The Edale Valley is situated just north of the Hope Valley and is easily accessible from the main A6187 road in Hope, or from Mam Nick on the Rushup Edge road west of Mam Tor.

WHEN TO WALK IT

This is a great outing all year round, although as the plateau is a raised blanket bog it is best avoided after prolonged periods of rain.

It is best avoided in bad weather which can hang around on the plateau. The reduced (and at times zero) visibility and lack of landmarks make it easy to get lost on the plateau.

TERRAIN AND NAVIGATION

There are steep paths and rocky sections on the ascent, descent and along the edge, and the section through the Woolpacks can be particularly boggy following wet weather. It is advisable to carry map and

The Woolpacks on a fine summer day.

compass, and to know how to use them.

FACILITIES AND REFRESHMENTS

There are toilets at the car park and at the Edale visitor centre. The visitor centre also has a shop and can provide local information; it's next to the Fieldhead Campsite. The Penny Pot Cafe by Edale station is perfectly placed for pre- or post-walk refreshments. There's also a cafe at Newfold Farm further into the village, as well as a general store. There are also a couple of pubs in the village – the Rambler Inn and the Old Nags Head

DOGS AND KIDS

Livestock and ground-nesting birds mean Kinder is a dog-on-lead kind of place, particularly between 1 March and 31 July when it is the law under the CRoW Act that dogs must be on short leads.

This walk is a great choice for fit and

adventurous youngsters, who will really enjoy the boulders. It's quite an energetic walk so pack extra snacks and water. There is the option to turn back down Jacob's Ladder as an escape route.

POINTS OF INTEREST

The bridge at the foot of Jacob's Ladder form part of a packhorse route from Hayfield to Edale, a trade route for lead, coal, salt and wool from mediaeval times until the railway was opened in 1894.

Edale Cross, thought to be mediaeval, is a boundary cross and guidestone at the top of the ancient packhorse route.

Interesting rock formations including the anvil-shaped Noe Stool, the giant gritstone outcrop of the Pagoda, and a large cluster of curiously shaped boulders known as the Woolpacks, all formed by weathering and erosion on the moors.

14km/8.7 miles

11/ HOPE STATION TO EDALE STATION

A high-level linear walk from Hope train station to Edale train station via Win Hill and Kinder Scout, visiting Hope Cross along a historical trade route.

/ ESSENTIAL INFO
GRADE ● ● ● ○
DISTANCE **14KM/8.7 MILES**
ASCENT **570M**
TIME **5 HRS (WALKER)/2.5 HRS (RUNNER)**
START/FINISH **HOPE/EDALE**
START GRID REF **SK 181 832**
START GPS **53.3456, -1.7293**
OS MAP **OL1 THE PEAK DISTRICT: DARK PEAK AREA (1:25,000)**

/ OVERVIEW
This is a grand day out so long as you have lots of energy and plenty of food and water in your rucksack! It takes in some of the best views in the Dark Peak, so save it for a day with excellent visibility. This route climbs steeply from Hope train station to Win Hill, then descends a sloping ridge more gently towards Hope Cross before climbing again on to the quieter eastern side of Kinder Scout. From here, the path works south-west along the edge before dropping down to The Nab and into Edale. In the late summer months you can enjoy the dazzling purple heather and edible juicy bilberries. A hard day on your legs, but worth it for the views!

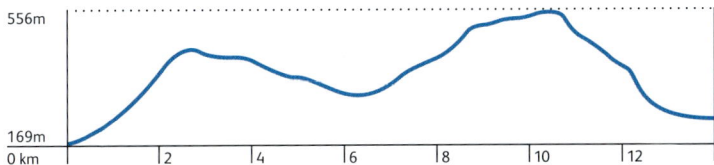

Looking back through the trees before heading up Crookstone Hill.

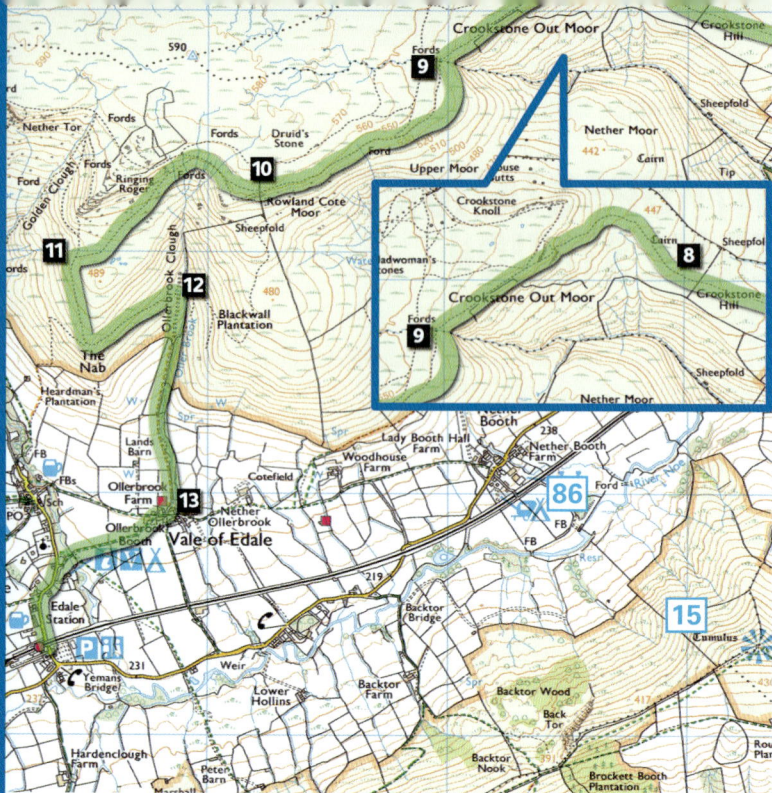

| DIRECTIONS

S From platform 2 (Manchester–Sheffield trains) at Hope station, walk up the first set of steps of the railway bridge and then **turn immediately left** to walk straight back down a set of steps (don't cross over to the other side of the railway bridge). Join the footpath on the **right** between a set of railings for approximately 50m.

From platform 1 (Sheffield–Manchester trains) at Hope station, or the station car park, take the steps up the railway bridge and cross the footbridge, then walk down the steps straight ahead of you (don't take the steps on the left that take you to platform 2). Join the footpath on the **right** between a set of railings for approximately 50m.

2 At the end of the railings, **turn left** through a gate and follow the path gradually uphill through open pasture for approximately 700m, keeping the river on your right.

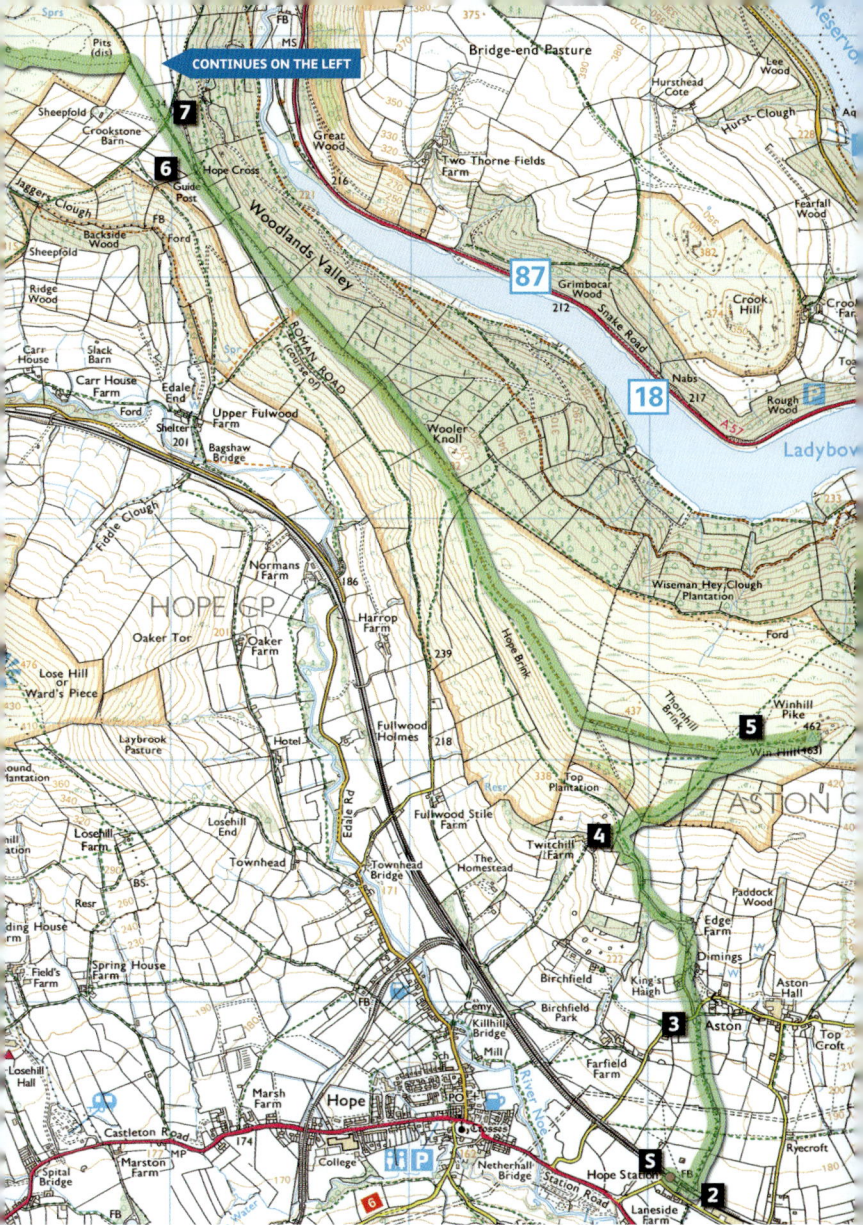

CONTINUES ON THE LEFT

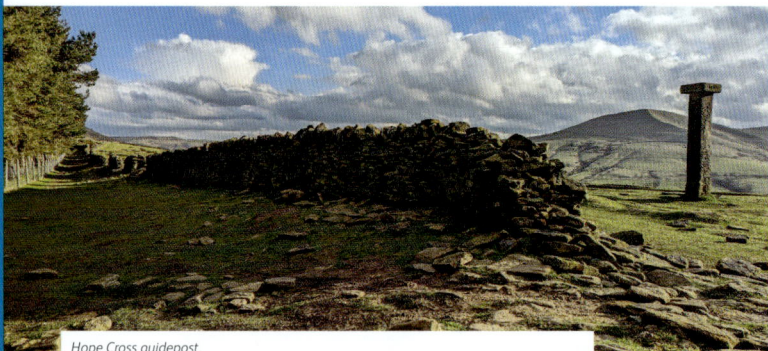
Hope Cross guidepost.

3 At Aston Lane (a road), **turn left** and then **almost immediately right** to leave the road and join a lane heading uphill. After approximately 400m along the lane, **turn left** where it ends and join a signposted bridleway lined with trees. This section feels like going back in time as you walk between moss-covered drystone walls and pass the ruins of a large barn. Keep the line of trees close to your left after the barn ruins for about 200m.

4 At the gate (SK 178 847) take a breather to prepare yourself for the steep climb ahead. **Turn sharp right** (north-east) and walk steeply uphill along a grassy path through the middle of the field towards a metal gate. Go through the gate and follow the path steeply uphill for about 400m. The rocky outcrop of Winhill Pike will gradually come into view ahead of you. At the signpost (SK 184 850) there is the option to walk up to the summit trig of Winhill Pike before heading towards Kinder Scout. It's certainly worth it for panoramic views on a clear day, including Ladybower Reservoir to the north, the Great Ridge to the west, Kinder Scout to the north-west, and Stanage Edge to the east.

> **Winhill Pike:** If visibility is good, you may wish to bag the trig on Winhill Pike, or just to take in the views. Just past the signpost (SK 184 850), turn right to follow the path up towards the rocky summit. Go left where the path splits, gradually ascending towards the top. There's a direct and easy scramble to the trig pillar, or you can loop back to it along the path of the rocky outcrop. If it's not too windy, it's a lovely spot for a brew and a snack. Otherwise, it's best to wait until you drop down towards the woods for shelter. After your summit-bagging photos, head back down the same way to signpost no. 25.

5 Follow the signpost directions towards Wooler Knoll (west at first and then veering north-west) along a broad footpath that very gradually descends for approximately 2km, before meeting a long fenced line of trees and a derelict stone wall (don't head into the woods here unless you need a sheltered lunch break). Continue descending, keeping the line of trees on your right for about 1.6km until you reach a tall stone guidepost to the left. This is Hope Cross, marking the crossroads of four historical packhorse routes.

6 Go through the gap in the derelict stone wall to take a closer look at the Hope Cross, then head through the large metal gate behind it and follow a footpath for 250m towards a cluster of signposts next to a stile and a gate (SK 159 876). Cross the stile to reach the junction of crossroads.

> If visibility is poor you may wish to take the lower path that skirts around the eastern edge of Kinder Scout via Edale YHA. This is not exactly a shortcut but offers less harsh conditions in challenging weather. After crossing the stile turn left and follow the signposted public bridleway to Edale. This route undulates up and down quite a bit before reaching the hostel, including a short steep section after Jaggers Clough, but it's a good option if you don't want to go up Kinder Scout. Watch out for mountain bikes! Keep to the bridleway until you get to a signpost marking the way to the youth hostel. There's still quite a bit of walking to go as the hostel isn't in Edale village. When you reach the YHA, walk to its far side, go through a gate and along the grassy path through a field (don't drop down to the road from the YHA car park). The path takes you through a small wooded area before dropping down towards Ollerbrook Farm. In the farmyard the path splits – right takes you straight to the Nag's Head pub or Newfold Cafe, left takes you towards The Rambler Inn and the Penny Pot Cafe near the train station and car park.

7 At the path junction, **take the signposted public bridleway** towards Alport Bridge (north-west) for 300m. Cross the stile next to the gate, then immediately take a rough path to the **left (west)** that ascends the hill. After about 450m you will reach a stone post inscribed *Crookstone*, a signpost and two trees standing together. Picnic under the trees? From here you can look back to Win Hill, with Ladybower Reservoir still in sight to the left. After a rest, it'll be time to hike up Kinder Scout so get the jelly babies ready!

Looking to Kinder Scout from Hope Brink.

8 **Continue north-west** along the grassy moorland path that takes you gently uphill towards Kinder Scout. The path bends south-west as it joins the edge of Kinder Scout and eventually reaches a quarried rocky outcrop. Stay on the gradually ascending path along the edge for about 600m, until you reach a noticeable gully in the hillside – Jaggers Clough (SK 139 877).

9 **Cross the gully** via rocks (the water in the ford often dries up after prolonged dry spells) and continue along the edge path, enjoying the views, for about 1.1km until you reach a junction of paths (SK 132 872).

10 **Take the path to the right** to stay up high and continue for about 300m as the path gradually bends to the left, crossing shallow fords which may or may not have water in depending on the time of year. **Turn left** at the next junction of paths, heading downhill through rough moorland ground. Watch out for the grouse that might leap out in front of you! There is plenty of purple heather and bilberries (smaller and slightly more sour than blueberries) in August and September here.

11 **Turn left** at the T-junction, heading away from Ringing Roger and down towards The Nab. After walking down a few rough steps, take a look at the view of Edale below from the rocky outcrop of The Nab. Facing towards the Great Ridge on the other side of the valley, **turn left** and follow a grassy path down towards Ollerbrook Clough. Yes – this is the scenic route back to Edale!

12 As you get closer to Ollerbrook Clough, follow the path that zigzags steeply to the right, keeping the stream on your left. Go through the gate and follow the path through open pasture towards houses and a farm, keeping the stone wall closely on your left.

13 **Turn right** at the lane to enter Ollerbrook farmyard. From here, **take the right fork** along a track to the Old Nag's Head and Newfold Farm cafe, **or the left fork** along a track to the Rambler Inn and Penny Pot Cafe by the train station. Catch a train to Hope to collect your car or head straight home!

| GOOD TO KNOW

PUBLIC TRANSPORT AND ACCESS

Hope sits on the Manchester–Sheffield railway line and is well served by trains daily.

There is a car park at Hope station with 10 spaces. There are a few additional lay-bys on Station Road. If parking isn't possible next to Hope train station then try the pay & display car park on Castleton Road in the centre of Hope village; it's a 15-minute walk back to the start of the route. This car park has public toilets.

Bus service 271/272 links Sheffield with Hope.

If arriving by road, note that Winnats Pass is sometimes closed after snow or in icy conditions.

WHEN TO WALK IT

This is a great outing all year round, although as the Kinder Scout plateau is a raised blanket bog it is best avoided after prolonged periods of rain.

It is best avoided in bad weather which can hang around on the plateau. Reduced (and at times zero) visibility and lack of landmarks on the Kinder Scout section could make this a bleak walk, so check the forecast carefully before

heading out and remember your map and compass.

TERRAIN AND NAVIGATION

There are steep paths and rocky sections on the ascent, descent and along the edge, and the moorland section is exposed to the elements. It is advisable to carry a map and compass, and to know how to use them.

FACILITIES AND REFRESHMENTS

There are toilets on the trains between Manchester and Sheffield, but not at Hope station. There are facilities, refreshments and a small shop in Hope village, a 30-minute round trip on foot from the station.

There are toilets at the car park and the visitor centre at Edale. The visitor centre also has a shop and can provide local information. The Penny Pot Cafe by Edale station is perfectly placed for pre- or post-walk refreshments and has a toilet. There's also a cafe at Newfold Farm next to the general store. There are even a couple of pubs – the Rambler Inn and the Old Nags Head.

DOGS AND KIDS

Livestock and ground-nesting birds mean this route is a dog-on-lead kind of place, particularly between 1 March and 31 July when

it is the law under the CRoW Act that dogs must be on short leads.

This walk is eminently escapable at most points simply by turning back or taking a lower route. The alternative option is to miss out Crookstone Hill, and take the lower route to Edale via the youth hostel or even drop down to Hope Road. You will still be able to enjoy the Kinder experience as you skirt around its foothills.

POINTS OF INTEREST

Hope is one of England's oldest villages, pre-dating the *Domesday Book*. Since the 19th century it has been a centre of industry, historically with the Pindale Lead Mine and more recently with the largest cement plant in the UK, which you can see from this route.

Howden and Derwent dams were constructed in the early 20th century to supply water to Sheffield and cities in the Midlands. Ladybower Reservoir opened in 1945.

Hope Cross is a tall pillar with a square capstone dated 1737 inscribed with the names of Shefield (sic), Glossop, Edale and Hope. Located at the crossroads of four packhorse routes, it was originally erected as a mediaeval boundary marker for the Peak Forest.

17km / 10.6 miles

12 / EDALE TO KINDER GATES

A high-level circular walk from Edale up on to the Kinder plateau via Kinder Gates, visiting the highest waterfall in the Peak District.

/ ESSENTIAL INFO

GRADE ●●●○

DISTANCE **17KM/10.6 MILES**
ASCENT **636M**
TIME **6 HRS (WALKER)/3.5 HRS (RUNNER)**
START/FINISH **EDALE**
START GRID REF **SK 123 853**
START GPS **53.3648, -1.8160**
OS MAP **OL1 THE PEAK DISTRICT: DARK PEAK AREA (1:25,000)**

/ OVERVIEW

A true Kinder experience – be prepared to get your feet wet! This route follows a good path along the start of the Pennine Way up Jacob's Ladder to Edale Rocks, then continues to Kinder Low trig point and the head of Kinder Downfall. It then follows a short section of the River Kinder into the moorland plateau, characterised by peat groughs and boggy conditions underfoot. After visiting the giant boulders of Kinder Gates along the river, it heads to the top of Crowden Brook on the southern rim of the plateau along a vague path across the plateau where you'll need compass skills to navigate. It then works its way down Crowden Clough before returning to Edale village via gentler open pasture.

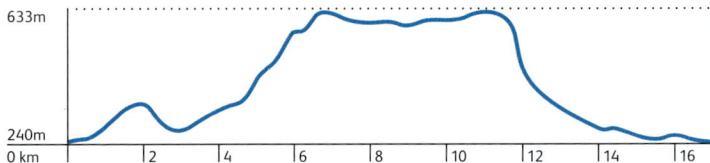

Kinder Downfall.

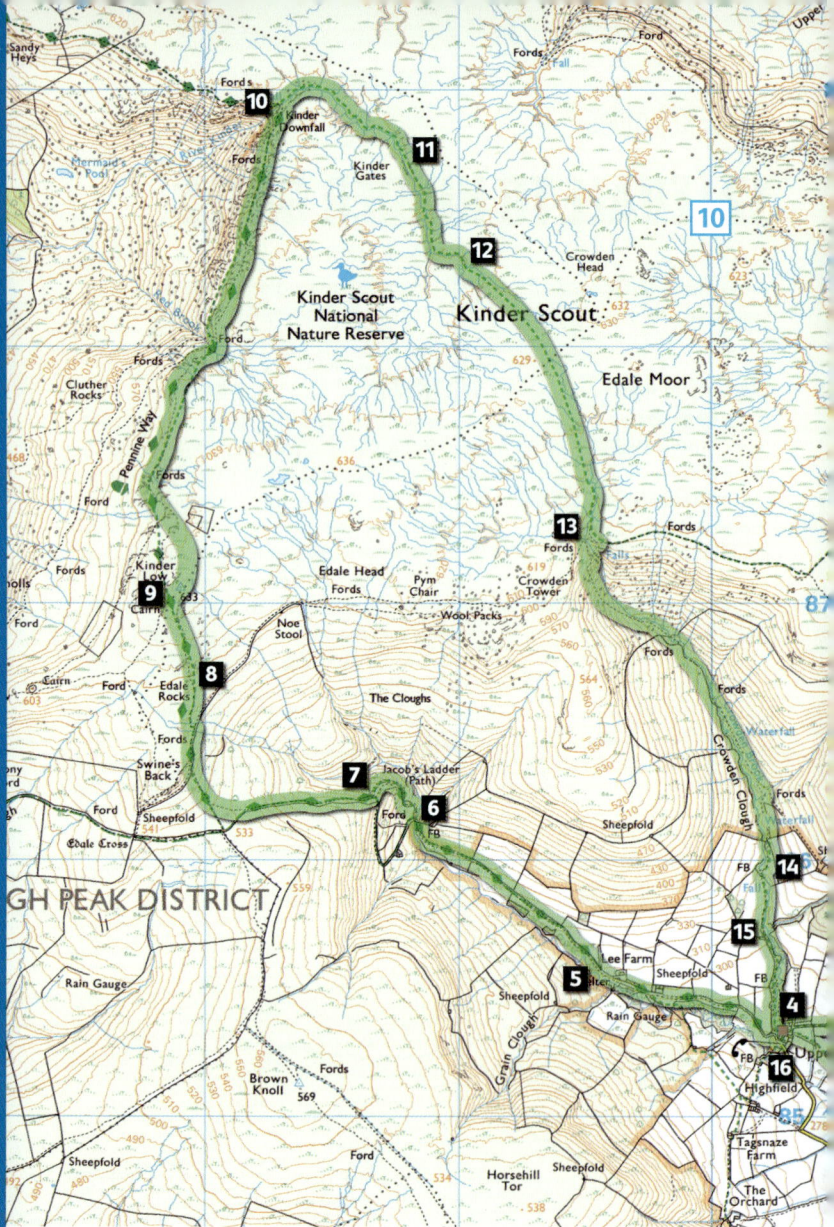

/ DIRECTIONS

S From underneath the railway bridge on the road into Edale village, head up into the village. Pass the visitor centre on your right and the church on your left. A short distance further on, and immediately before reaching the Old Nags Head, the Pennine Way is signed **left** on a fingerpost – take this narrow tree-lined footpath alongside a stream.

2 After 300m the path splits: **take the left** through the gate, following the signpost for the *Pennine Way*. Keep going for 900m through open pasture and listen out for the call of the curlew if you're walking this route in the spring or summer. There's a good bench for a sit along the way, looking out towards Mam Tor.

3 After going through a gate the path briefly ascends more steeply. Go straight on, walking towards a drystone wall with a gate in the middle. Go through the gate and descend the path that winds between two hillocks. After another gate you will pass a ruined farm building on your left. Continue along the footpath towards the farm and houses at Upper Booth.

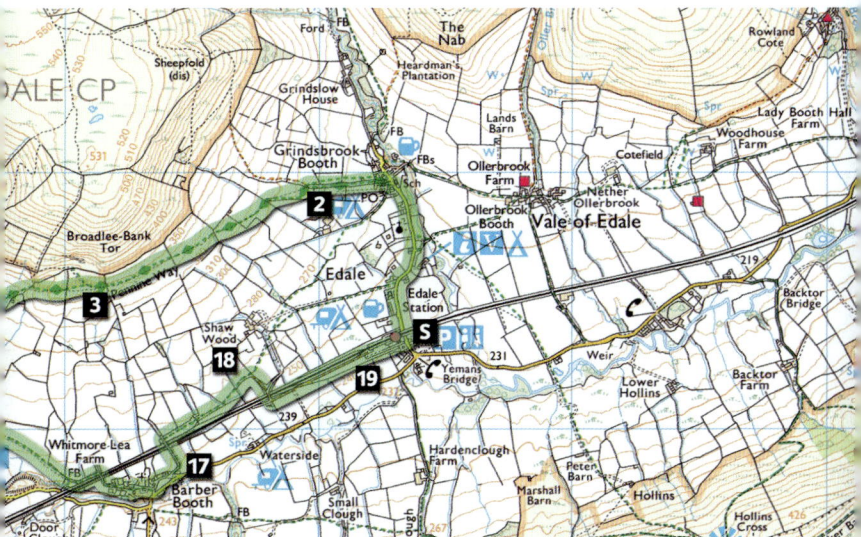

4 At the end of the footpath, go through the gate that brings you to a T-junction. **Turn left** along the lane and walk through Upper Booth hamlet and farmyard. **Turn right** on to the road and follow it to Lee Farm where there are a few houses and farm outbuildings (ignore the sign on the metal gate that says *Residents only beyond this point* as this only applies to vehicles, not walkers). Pass the houses at Lee Farm and before going through the gate ahead, note the National Trust barn on the left which has a public information display and is a really good shelter from the rain or wind if you need a tea break.

5 Go through the gate and continue along the track until you reach a narrow stone bridge over the River Noe. Cross the bridge and if the sun is shining consider sitting on the riverbank for tea and snacks – you've got a steep climb up Jacob's Ladder coming up next! While you sit and listen to the cascades, imagine lines of packhorses and their drivers or 'jaggers' passing through here along the historical trade route between Edale and Hayfield on the way to Stockport.

6 From the National Trust sign for *Jacob's Ladder*, ascend the steep staircase on the **right**. This was named after Jacob Marshall, who created the original shortcut up the bank in the 18th century for him to walk up while his pack-horses were sent up the gentler winding track – now a bridleway busy with mountain bikes. It's quite a slog up the staircase so take your time. Eventually there is a large stone cairn where you can have a rest and enjoy the reward of the climb – a great view!

> If the weather is poor, you may wish to turn back and retrace your steps at this point because the Kinder plateau is exposed to the elements and can be tricky to navigate in low visibility.

7 From the cairn, follow the steep bridleway ascending west for about 500m. At the junction, **turn right** to follow a flagstone path uphill. This joins a rocky path that skirts the hillside of Swine's Back on the left. This soon becomes a flagstone path again, passing two small cairns. At the third larger cairn take the path to the **left** to ascend the flagstone path up to the giant boulders of Edale Rocks (SK 079 867). This is a great spot for a brew and a snack with a spectacular view of the Edale Valley to the east, and the rocks provide a good wind shelter if needed.

The packhorse bridge at the foot of Jacob's Ladder.

8 With Edale Rocks to your left, continue along the path heading north towards Kinder Low trig point. The path brings you to a point between a large cairn and the trig point – **veer right** to reach the trig point upon a large boulder (SK 079 870). If the weather is good, check out the panoramic views!

9 Pick up the wide path **heading north** from the trig point (not shown as a path on the OS map but it's obvious and well used). After 250m the path drops down slightly towards a large cairn (SK 078 873) – **veer left** to take this. After the cairn, **turn right** to follow the rocky plateau edge path for 1.6km towards the top of Kinder Downfall. It winds and wanders between low-lying rocks, so if in doubt, **walk on a bearing of 20°** until you reach the River Kinder at the head of Kinder Downfall (SK 083 889).

> If the weather is poor and you're not confident with your map and compass skills, you may wish to turn back and retrace your steps at this point because the Kinder plateau is exposed to the elements and can be tricky to navigate in low visibility.

Kinder Gates in a winter coat.

10 **Turn right** on to a path alongside the river, heading into the moorland plateau (don't cross to the other side of the river). Follow this for 600m. The path is patchy at best and you need to be prepared to get your feet wet as you find your own way. Two giant boulders will come into view on either side of the river – this is Kinder Gates (SK 087 886). Unless the water is really low or dried up, you'll need to step up on to the peaty grough on the right and walk to the large boulder stone. This provides a handy viewing platform for lunch. While here, get your compass ready for the next moorland section.

11 Continue along the right-hand side of the river, **walking on a bearing of 160°** for 300m until you reach a fork in the river (SK 088 883), which may be dry depending on recent rainfall. **Turn left** along this tributary, heading east for 100m. Nip up along the stream bank if it's too wet underfoot and look out for a large cairn (SK 090 883).

12 From the cairn, **walk on a bearing of 128°** (south-east) for 300m where you might be able to pick up a patchy trod. This is when the fun really begins with groughs and bogs to navigate over/around! Mountain hares might be spotted. After 300m, **change to a bearing of 160°** and continue walking across the moor for about 900m to reach the southern edge of the plateau. You are aiming to drop down to the ford at the head of Crowden Brook (SK 094 872) – good luck! If you miss this, get to the southern edge path (if in doubt just head south until you reach the plateau edge) and walk along to the ford.

> If you've ended up too far east along the southern edge of the plateau, it is possible to walk back down to Edale via Grindsbrook Clough from the ford head (SK 105 872) – an easy grade-1 scramble but slow going, or Grindslow Knoll (SK 109 868) – a steep descent with a bit of scrambling initially.

13 **Cross the ford** at the head of Crowden Brook (SK 094 872), looking out towards the Mam Tor ridge with the water flowing down to the left (unless it has dried up) and the boulders of Crowden Tower above to the right. Take the rough trod that heads south beside the stream and follow it round to the right. Where it forks (SK 095 871), **turn left** to take the steep way down the clough. It's rough going at first and can't really be called a path but it does improve with descent. In late summer you can feast on bilberries on the way. Follow the course of the brook down, choosing your own route where the path is unclear (you may need to switch sides of the brook a couple of times) until you reach a more defined footpath (SK 096 869). **Cross the brook** to join a path that heads south for 600m, walking parallel with the flow of water to the right until you reach a gate into a small woodland (SK 101 859).

14 Go through the gate into the small woodland, then cross the footbridge and **turn left** to go through a large wooden gate that leads into open pasture. Follow the grassy path for 250m. Head over the stile and follow the path past a large barn on the right. Continue for another 200m to reach a short set of steep steps on the left. **Take care** when descending the uneven steps, especially after rain. Follow the path through the woodland, which really comes to life with wild flowers during spring. Watch your footing as some sections of the path have partially fallen away.

15 Go through the gate at the end of the woodland path and **turn left** on to the lane to head over the footbridge and up to Upper Booth. **Turn left** into Upper Booth and walk through the yard past the farm outbuildings. Walk through the wide gate opening (the gate is usually open but there are steps on the left if it's shut) and look out for the signpost on the left marking a public footpath (SK 103 853). **Turn right** to take the public footpath, going through a gate into open pasture.

River Kinder from the top of the Downfall.

16 As you walk through the fields, which often contain livestock, you'll cross two short stone bridges, a wooden bridge and a larger railway bridge that takes you into the hamlet of Barber Booth. Follow the track through the farm buildings and houses of Barber Booth. Shortly after passing a Methodist chapel on the left, the track meets a T-junction. **Turn left** to walk along the lane for about 80m, then **turn left** to leave the lane and join a track (if you end up on the road then you need to backtrack a few steps).

17 Follow the track over the railway bridge. **Turn right** through the gate and follow the path. After the next gate, follow the path to the **right** alongside the edge of the field parallel with the train tracks. Continue on the path through more fields until you reach a signposted concession path. **Take the right turn** towards Edale station.

18 Head through a couple of gates to meet a gravel track, then continue on to cross the railway bridge and follow the bend to the left. When the gravel track meets a field, follow the signposted path towards Edale station across the field, walking parallel to the train tracks which are now on your left.

19 When you reach a short wooden fence at the end of the path, **turn left** through a gate into a small woodland, then almost immediately **turn right** towards Edale station car park. If you have time for a brew or an ice cream, the Penny Pot Cafe is conveniently located just past the Edale station entrance.

GOOD TO KNOW

PUBLIC TRANSPORT AND ACCESS

Edale sits on the Manchester–Sheffield railway line and is well-served by trains daily.

There are pay & display car parks in Edale village and at the station; these can fill up early on fine weather weekends. The Edale Valley is situated just north of the Hope Valley and is easily accessible from the main A6187 road in Hope, or from Mam Nick on the Rushup Edge road west of Mam Tor.

WHEN TO WALK IT

This is a great outing all year round, although as the plateau is a raised blanket bog it is best avoided after prolonged periods of rain. The route is best in spring and summer after a dry spell because conditions underfoot are better and there are moorland plants to enjoy including cottongrass, rosebay willowherb, and cloudberry flowers.

It is best avoided in bad weather. The reduced (and at times zero) visibility and lack of landmarks on the plateau make this a dull and possibly dangerous walk in such conditions – even for those proficient with map and compass.

TERRAIN AND NAVIGATION

There are steep paths and rocky sections on the ascent, descent and along the edge, and the moorland section is exposed with faint paths/trods. Take care with navigation on the moorland plateau which is characterised by a maze of groughs where you can easily become disoriented or lost. If in doubt, head south across the plateau to pick up the edge path. It is advisable to carry a map and compass, and to know how to use them.

FACILITIES AND REFRESHMENTS

There are toilets at the car park and at the Edale visitor centre. The visitor centre also has a shop and can provide local information; it's next to the Fieldhead Campsite. The Penny Pot Cafe by Edale station is perfectly placed for pre- or post-walk refreshments. There's also a cafe at Newfold Farm further into the village, as well as a general store. There are also a couple of pubs in the village – the Rambler Inn and the Old Nags Head.

DOGS AND KIDS

Livestock and ground-nesting birds mean Kinder is a dog-on-lead kind of place, particularly between 1 March and 31 July when it is the law under the CRoW Act that dogs must be on short leads.

This walk is a great choice for adventurous kids because there are boulders and a trig point to clamber on, and water for paddling in, but it's quite long and tough going for little legs. Shorten the route by turning back at the top of Jacob's Ladder or at Kinder Downfall, or miss out Kinder Downfall and head east on bearing 104° from Kinder Low trig point to Noe Stool (an anvil-shaped boulder) to cut across to the edge path back to Edale, via Crowden Clough or Grindslow Knoll. This is well trodden but boggy after heavy rain.

POINTS OF INTEREST

The source of the River Noe is at Edale Head where it runs down the clough alongside the Jacob's Ladder footpath and through the Vale of Edale. The former cotton mill in Edale was originally powered by the Noe until it was converted to steam power.

The River Kinder is approximately 3 miles (4.8km) long, flowing to its confluence with the River Sett at Bowden Bridge (a grade-II listed packhorse bridge) through the Kinder Gates rocks, over Kinder Downfall and through Kinder Reservoir.

12km / 7.5 miles

13 / EDALE TO DRAGON RAPIDE AIRCRAFT WRECK & SEAL STONES

A high-level circular walk from Edale up on to the Kinder plateau via Grindslow Knoll, visiting an aircraft wreck and Seal Stones, with two plateau crossings.

/ ESSENTIAL INFO

GRADE ●●●○

DISTANCE **12 KM/7.5 MILES**

ASCENT **400M**

TIME **4.5 HRS (WALKER)/2 HRS (RUNNER)**

START/FINISH **EDALE**

START GRID REF **SK 123 853**

START GPS **53.3648, -1.8160**

OS MAP **OL1 THE PEAK DISTRICT: DARK PEAK AREA (1:25,000)**

/ OVERVIEW

This starts out as a classic walk on Kinder but then wanders off into the moorland. It's worth waiting for a day with low wind in spring or summer so that the gentle call of the golden plover can be heard on the plateau. The route climbs quickly and steeply out of Edale on to Grindslow Knoll, winds around to the head of Grindsbrook Clough, then heads north along the edge of the plateau and follows the second arm of Grinds Brook into the moorland, visiting the remains of a small stone cabin and an aircraft site at Wove Hill. It then crosses the plateau to Seal Stones on the northern edge of Kinder Scout and works south to the head of Blackden Brook before a second (shorter) plateau crossing and a descent into Edale via The Nab.

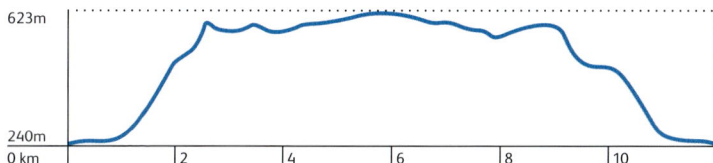

Edale in full bloom at the start of the ascent up Grindslow Knoll.

| DIRECTIONS

S From underneath the railway bridge on the road into Edale village, head up into the village. Pass the visitor centre on your right and the church on your left. A short distance further on, and immediately before reaching the Old Nags Head, the Pennine Way is signed **left** on a fingerpost – **take** this tree-lined footpath alongside a stream.

2 After 300m the path splits; **take the right fork**, following the signposted grassland path up towards Grindslow Knoll. After going through a gate, continue along the steep path for about 600m, watching out for loose rocks underfoot. After the next gate, continue on the same path, which becomes even steeper with some steps and then rocks to clamber over. As the climbing ends, **fork left** as you top out on the highest point of Grindslow Knoll (SK 109 868). From here, pick up the trod that briefly descends **north-west** to meet the edge path. Continue **north-west** on the edge path and walk to the head of Grinds Brook. Tea break?

3 **Cross the narrow ford** at the head of Grinds Brook to keep on the edge path heading north. Walk along the path for about 400m until you reach the next wide ford, characterised by a prominent rocky gorge (SK 106 876).

> If visibility is poor, you may wish to continue along the edge path to return to Edale. (Don't take the gorge route down as this is a steep, rocky descent and involves scrambling in places.) After crossing the ford, turn sharp right to walk south-east along the edge path for 250m. Continue on the same path as it bends north-east for another 250m, and then heads east for about 1.8km to a narrow ford at the top of Golden Clough. After crossing the ford walk over to the large cairn. Now jump to route direction numbers 9–11 below to return to Edale village.

4 Follow the river (or the riverbed if there's no water flowing) up into the moorland in a northerly and then north-westerly direction. There is a rough path to the left of the river initially, then to the right after the first bend. Find your way along the river until you reach the remains of Four Jacks Cabin (SK 103 879), so named because it was repaired by four men named Jack in the 1930s. The remaining stone walls serve as quite a nice sheltered seat and mug rest.

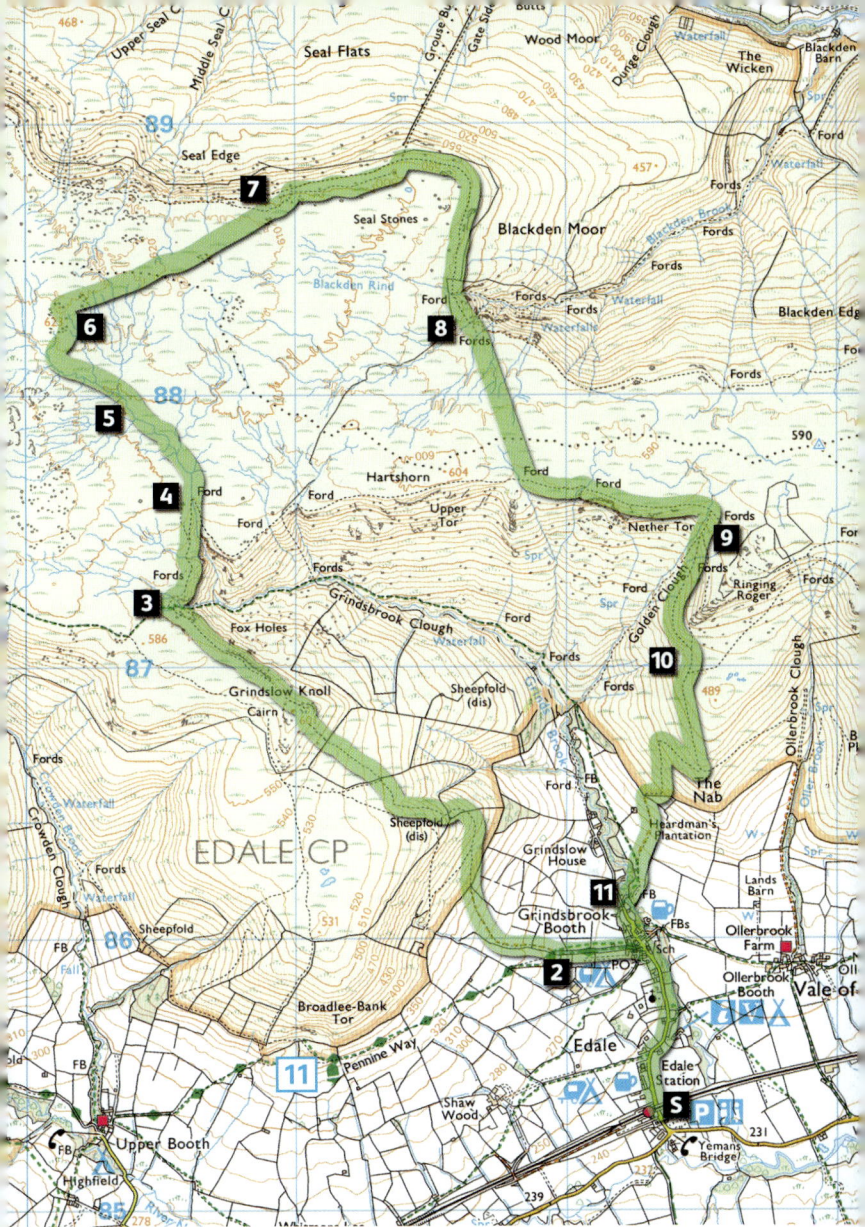

The remains of Four Jacks Cabin.

5 Continue to follow the river for about 300m, reaching a tributary to the right (SK 100 881). From here **walk on a bearing of 29°** for about 100m, following the tributary initially and then breaking away to follow a grough towards some large scattered rocks. Before walking up to the rocky high point of the landscape, known as Wove Hill, look out for the aircraft remains of Dragon Rapide (SK 101 882). The plane crashed in 1963 following a photographic survey and both crew members survived (please leave all aircraft remains as you found them). Then find your way to the top of the slightly elevated moorland high point (marked as 623m on the Ordnance Survey map), where the large boulders provide a lovely peaceful spot to sit for lunch. In summer and spring you might be able to hear the gentle call of the golden plover.

6 **Walk on a bearing of 69°** for about 800m across the moorland between peat hags, towards the northern edge of the Kinder plateau. If you walk quietly you might spot a mountain hare sunbathing in a grough, and there are plenty of mosses and lichen to notice en route too. On reaching a cluster of boulders (SK 109 886) the northern edge comes into view in good weather. This is another good lunch spot.

Moorland at the head of Grinds Brook.

7 **Walk on a bearing of 40°** for about 100m to pick up a path along the
northern edge of the plateau. **Turn right** on to the path to follow it east for
about 600m. The path is inconsistent in sections, especially around the large
boulders. Continue along the edge path as it bends around to the south for
about 400m towards Blackden Brook. Go through the gate and walk to the
second ford of Blackden Brook (SK 116 882).

8 **Turn right** here into the heather-clad moorland to walk **south on a bearing of
160°** for about 600m. This is known as the 'seven-minute crossing' between the
northern and southern edges of Kinder Scout, though it takes a little longer from
north to south. It is pathless but well trodden so you may well see boot prints
in the peat. Aim to pop out on the southern edge path at SK 118 876. **Turn
left** on to the flagstone path, heading east for about 200m towards the rocky
outcrop of Nether Tor. Note the bench-like boulder at SK 120 876 overlooking
Edale Valley and offering a great spot to finish your flask. From here, continue
along the edge path for 400m to a point where the path begins to descend
more steeply at SK 124 875. **Turn right** here to follow an initially bouldery
path that turns into a few steps down towards a narrow ford and a large cairn.

Looking back along the southern edge of the plateau.

9 Cross the narrow ford to reach the cairn (SK 125 875), walk around to the right of it and **turn right** to follow the steep path down. Soon you'll have the rocky outcrop of Ringing Roger towering over you to the left. This path becomes overgrown with ferns in summer so if in doubt **walk on a bearing of 200°** from the cairn for the first 300m, then on a **bearing of 148°** for the next 100m to meet a junction below Ringing Roger.

10 Continue south for about 400m towards The Nab. **Turn sharp right** after the short section of steps to follow the zigzagging path downhill towards Grinds Brook. After the gate follow the path through open pasture past an old guide-post to join a flagstone path. **Turn left** on to the path, walk past the stone barn, and follow the path round to meet a gate into a small woodland. Go down the steps, cross the bridge, and follow the path up to a stone track and a cottage.

11 **Turn left** to walk along the track towards Grindsbrook Booth and the Old Nags Head pub where you can grab a drink and a bite to eat. Other options include the Newfold Farm cafe, or follow the village road down towards Edale train station and the main car park where there's the Rambler Inn pub and the Penny Pot Cafe.

Edale sits on the Manchester–Sheffield railway line and is well served by trains daily.

There are pay & display car parks in Edale village and at the station. These can fill up early on fine weather weekends. The Edale Valley is situated just north of the Hope Valley and is easily accessible from the main A6187 road in Hope or from Mam Nick on the Rushup Edge road west of Mam Tor.

WHEN TO WALK IT

This is a great outing all year round in good weather. As the plateau is a raised blanket bog it is best avoided after prolonged periods of rain.

It is best avoided in bad weather which can hang around on the plateau. The reduced and at times zero visibility and lack of landmarks make this a dull and possibly dangerous walk in such conditions.

Aim for fair weather in spring and summer to enjoy the local flora and moorland bird life, most notably the golden plover which breed here.

TERRAIN AND NAVIGATION

There are steep paths and rocky sections on the ascent, descent and along the edge. The moorland section is exposed with faint paths/trods, and is at times pathless. It can be tough walking up and down the peat groughs. A map and compass is required for this walk.

FACILITIES AND REFRESHMENTS

There are toilets at the car park and at the Edale visitor centre. The visitor centre also has a shop and can provide local information; it's next to the Fieldhead campsite. The Penny Pot Cafe by Edale station is perfectly placed for pre- or post-walk refreshments. There's also a cafe and bistro at Newfold Farm further into the village, as well as a general store. There are also a couple of pubs in the village – the Rambler Inn and the Old Nags Head.

DOGS AND KIDS

Livestock and ground-nesting birds mean Kinder is a dog-on-lead kind of place, particularly between 1 March and 31 July when it is the law under the CRoW Act that dogs must be on short leads.

There is nothing especially dangerous about this walk as long as you know how to use a map and compass to navigate in case of low visibility. It is eminently escapable at most points by simply turning back or heading south towards the Edale side of the plateau. Fit youngsters will enjoy the maze of peat groughs and gritstone rocks. There is the option to miss out the aircraft wreck and the plateau crossings, and simply head east along the edge path from the top of the second arm of Grinds Brook to return to Edale village via Ringing Roger and The Nab.

POINTS OF INTEREST

Four Jacks Cabin was originally built around 1870 and was the highest shooting cabin in Derbyshire. It was rebuilt by four 'Jacks' from Edale in 1930, but now only part of the stone foundations remain.

The Dragon Rapide plane crashed in 1963 following a photographic survey and both crew members survived. For more information see **www.aircrashsites.co.uk/air-crash-sites-5**

The plateau crossing between the top of Blackden Brook to the southern edge is known as the 'seven-minute crossing' (three minutes for fell runners!) and traverses the narrowest part of the plateau.

15km / 9.3 miles

14 / FAIR BROOK & ASHOP CLOUGH

A high-level circular walk from Snake Pass up on to the Kinder plateau via Fair Brook, visiting the Boxing Glove Stones.

/ ESSENTIAL INFO

GRADE ●●●○

DISTANCE **15KM/9.3 MILES**

ASCENT **649M**

TIME **5 HRS (WALKER)/3.5 HRS (RUNNER)**

START/FINISH **HOPE WOODLAND CAR PARK AT BIRCHEN CLOUGH**

START GRID REF **SK 109 914**

START GPS **53.4198, -1.8371**

OS MAP **OL1 THE PEAK DISTRICT: DARK PEAK AREA (1:25,000)**

/ OVERVIEW

Although this walk starts from the busy A57/Snake Pass, it's not long before you leave it well and truly behind you. After the unavoidable road section, this route starts climbing fairly gently to begin with, becoming gradually steeper as you make your way up Fair Brook, then hangs a right and heads west along the northern edge of the Kinder plateau, visiting the impressive Boxing Glove Stones (you can't miss them) and briefly picking up a short section of the Pennine Way National Trail to drop you down to the head of the River Ashop. From here, it snakes alongside the river before reaching the Snake Plantation and eventually returning you to your car.

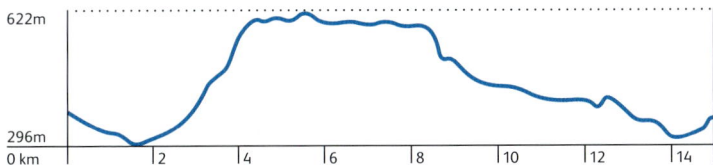

Clare Kelly looking down Fair Brook.

DIRECTIONS

S Directly from the car park, without crossing the road, **head south over a stile**. Follow the grassy track through the trees, parallel with the A57. When you get to the fork in the track, **bear right** to stay parallel to the road. Continue until the track meets the road at a lay-by.

2 **Take extra care** when you meet the road as it's often busy with fast motor-bikes and large vehicles. **Turn left** along the road, which has a grass verge for some of the way but unhelpfully not all of it: walk on the right-hand side of the road so you can face the oncoming traffic. After 700m, **turn right** through a gate to descend a path leading down to a footbridge. Cross the footbridge to reach a National Trust signpost for *Fair Brook*.

3 **Turn left** immediately after the footbridge, soon meeting the bottom of Fair Brook where you'll see another National Trust signpost. Start to ascend the path up Fair Brook, keeping the river to your left all the way up. There are some good pools at the lower end of the brook if you need to cool your feet down on a hot day, or even for a quick dip if you've remembered your towel. Look out for dippers bobbing up and down on the rocks nearby or searching for food underwater. The path becomes gradually steeper and rockier, eventually meeting a gate.

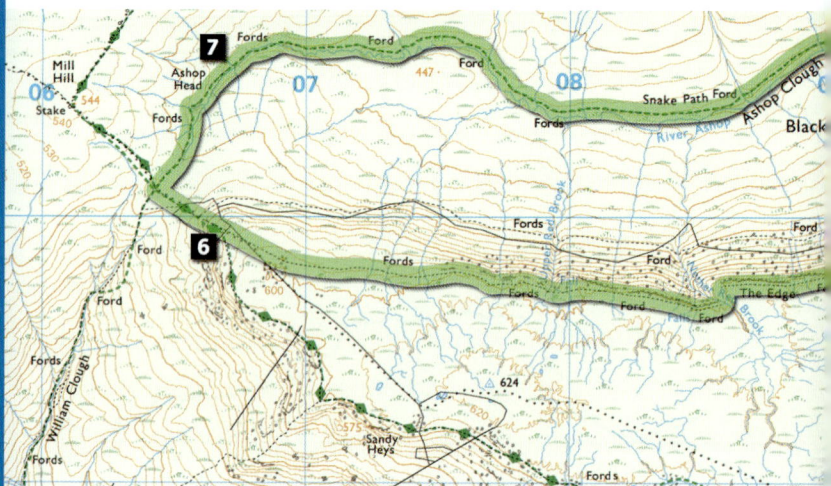

4 Go through the gate and stay on the same path, following the brook upwards through the rocks. After 300m the terrain levels out to reach the head of Fair Brook. If visibility is good, this is a marvellous spot to perch on a rock and admire the view of Alport Moor and Bleaklow on the other side of the Snake Pass. Tea break?

> If conditions and visibility are poor, you may wish to turn back and retrace your steps at this point because there is still a long walk ahead.

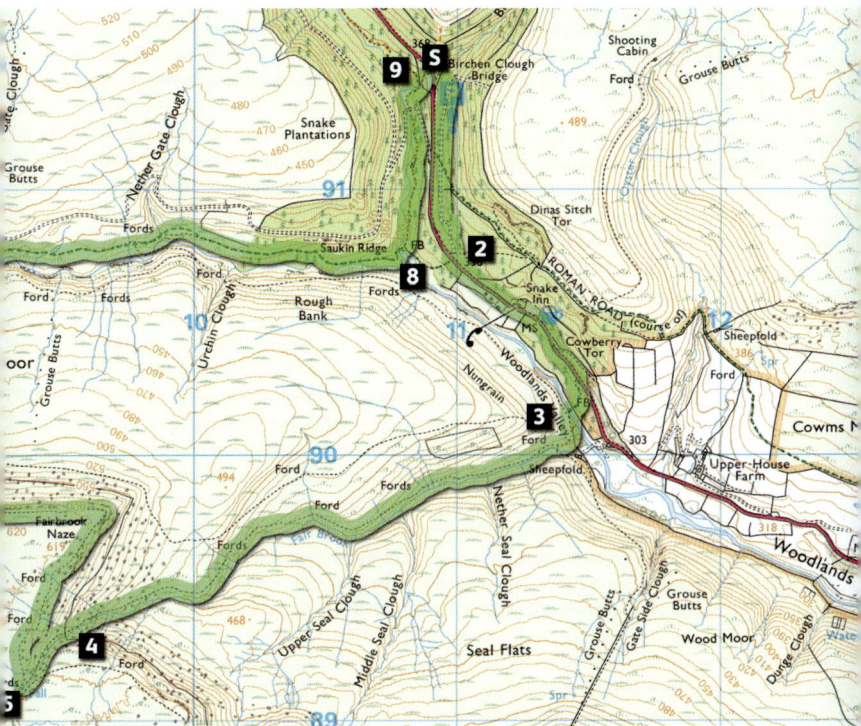

Ashop Clough in late summer.

5 **Turn sharp right** out of Fair Brook to follow a path that contours the edge of Kinder Scout in a Z-shape out to the spur of Fairbrook Naze. Keep to the high path along The Edge, which eventually brings Manchester into view. You'll step over several small streams that drop into the River Ashop below you, as well as pass huge gritstone boulders – can you spot the Boxing Glove Stones? Lunch here perhaps.

6 After about 4km you'll meet a junction with a wider path. If the fence is still there, you will have stepped over a stile before the final 150m. **Turn right** at this wide junction to briefly join the Pennine Way. Follow the wide path past the large cairn (SK 066 899), descending steeply along a flagged path. **Turn right** at the signpost, following the arrow that points towards the *Snake Inn* (this pub closed down in 2019).

7 This path is wet and muddy at first, but gradually becomes more defined and easier to walk along. It snakes alongside the River Ashop with superb views of the northern edge of Kinder Scout that you walked along earlier. You'll pass several fords, a cabin ruin and a footbridge across the river. After about 4.5km you'll reach a gate at the edge of the Snake Plantation. Go through the gate and continue along the same path through the plantation. Before the footbridge, there's a good river pool for a cold dip if you're brave enough!

8 Cross the footbridge and go straight through the gate, then follow the muddy path through the trees, with the stream to your left. Ignore the track that meets your path and the large bridge on the left; continue on the same path.

9 Cross the second footbridge and **turn right** to follow a rough path to a gate. Go through the gate and walk up the steps that zigzag towards the A57/Snake Pass. **Taking extra care here**, cross the road which brings you back to the car park.

GOOD TO KNOW

The 257 bus operated by Hulleys of Baslow runs on Sundays between Sheffield and Glossop over the Snake Pass. Check online for up-to-date information: *www.hulleys-of-baslow.co.uk*

The Hope Woodland car park located at Birchen Clough along the Snake Pass offers free parking. This can fill up quickly on weekends and any day during the summer holidays. There are also some lay-bys close to where the Snake Pass Inn pub used to be, but these also often fill up quickly. The car park is preferable for this circular route. The A57 (Snake Pass) between Glossop and Ladybower Reservoir is accessible from Manchester and Sheffield.

WHEN TO WALK IT

This route provides a particularly good day of walking in late spring and summer. In August and September, the sea of blooming heather along Ashop Clough is a sight to behold.

As the plateau is a raised blanket bog, it is best avoided after prolonged periods of rain. Good visibility is ideal, both for easy navigation and so you can enjoy the views.

TERRAIN AND NAVIGATION

There are steep paths and rocky sections on the ascent, descent and along the edge, and the northern edge is particularly exposed to the elements. Mobile phone reception is intermittent at best. It is advisable to carry a map and compass, and to know how to use them.

FACILITIES AND REFRESHMENTS

This route has no public facilities, so you will need to bring your own drinks, snacks and packed lunch. The Snake Inn no longer exists as a pub.

When nature calls, dig a hole at least 30m away from paths and water. Remember to bring a sealable bag with you and take all of your rubbish home with you, including toilet paper and sanitary items. If you're prepared to make a slight detour before or after your walk, the nearest public toilets are at Heatherdene car park (SK 202 859) which is open except in extreme weather conditions.

DOGS AND KIDS

Livestock and ground-nesting birds mean Kinder is a dog-on-lead kind of place, particularly between 1 March and 31 July when it is the law under the CRoW Act that dogs must be on short leads.

There is nothing especially dangerous about this walk but the full route is a long day out, especially for kids. You may be able to egg them on with the temptation of a swim in the River Ashop at the end. It is possible to turn back at the top of Fair Brook if legs are tired.

POINTS OF INTEREST

The Snake Pass was originally built as a Sheffield to Glossop turnpike to support faster transportation of materials for the cotton industry. It opened in 1821 and remains vulnerable to closures because of land slippage and snow.

The former Snake Pass Inn (originally known as Lady Clough House) was built in 1821 by the 6th Duke of Devonshire as a staging post for coach horses on the turnpike road. The name of the road is thought to derive from the Duke's snake emblem which welcomed visitors over the inn's front door.

Ashop Clough cabin (a substantial ruin) is thought to have been a shooting cabin. Grouse shooting became popular in the latter part of the 19th century and cabins were built close to the lines of shooting butts.

20km / 12.4 miles

15 / THREE TRIG PILLARS

A high-level circular walk from Edale up on to the Kinder plateau via Ringing Roger, visiting three trig pillars and Kinder Downfall, the Woolpacks and Crowden Tower.

/ ESSENTIAL INFO
GRADE ●●●○
DISTANCE **20KM/12.4 MILES**
ASCENT **708M**
TIME **7 HRS (WALKER)/3.5 HRS (RUNNER)**
START/FINISH **EDALE**
START GRID REF **SK 123 853**
START GPS **53.3648, -1.8160**
OS MAP **OL1 THE PEAK DISTRICT: DARK PEAK AREA (1:25,000)**

/ OVERVIEW
This is a big day out on Kinder Scout, so pack extra sandwiches! Bag three trig pillars and experience the flora and fauna that exists in the quieter reaches of the moor. This route climbs quickly and steeply out of Edale and bags the first trig pillar before heading along the northern edge of the plateau all the way to Upper Red Brook with stunning views of Alport Dale and Bleaklow, passing many curiously shaped rock formations. Then you get to bag the next two trig pillars in quicker succession and enjoy the view of Kinder Downfall before heading back to Edale via the Woolpacks and Grindslow Knoll.

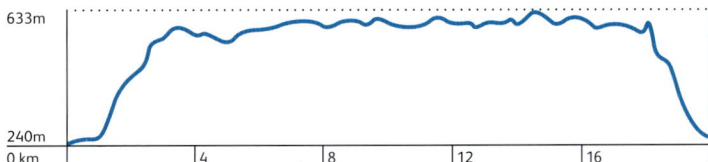

The lonely trig point on Edale Moor surrounded by cottongrass in June.

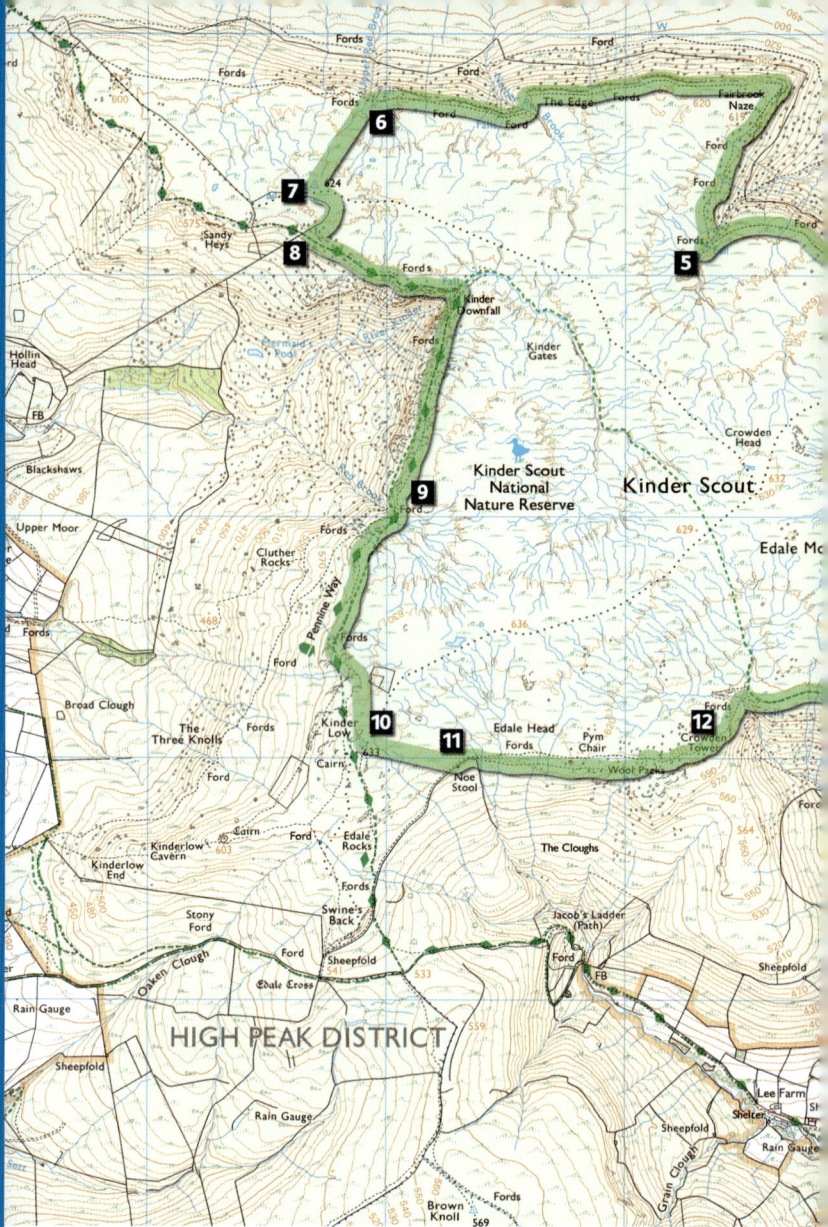

Early morning view in winter from the boulders at Ringing Roger.

| DIRECTIONS

S From underneath the railway bridge on the road into Edale village, head up into the village. Pass the visitor centre on your right and the church on your left. About 100m after passing the Old Nags Head pub the road changes from tarmac to unsurfaced track. A short distance further on, immediately before white iron gates, a footpath is signed **right** into the woods – **take this**, cross the river via the footbridge, then climb out the other side and follow the paved path into open pasture alongside the woods.

2 After 100m the path splits just after passing a small stone barn on the left: **keep right** and trend uphill through a gate, zigzagging left and right up the path on to The Nab. At a viewpoint over Edale, **cut back sharp left** up the rough steps, then follow the path north towards the Kinder plateau. The rocky outcrop of Ringing Roger will appear ahead. **Turn right** where the path forks, climbing up the steps towards Ringing Roger. When you reach the rocky climb to your right (SK 124 871), aim to follow the line of most resistance almost directly up the nose (the path was repaired relatively recently), passing several interesting boulders until you eventually reach the edge path which runs along the plateau rim.

3 Pick up the good path heading **north-east**. You will soon meet a series of small fords at the top of Oller Brook (these dry up sometimes). At the second ford (SK 128 873), turn **left** to follow a narrow path into the moorland for 50m. **Turn left** at the next ford (SK 129 874) to follow it deeper into the moor for 100m. Where the ford bends to the right (SK 129 875), get your compass out to **walk on a bearing of 353°** (north) for 250m across open moorland to the first trig pillar. Watch your footing as this area of moorland is a boot-swallowing bogland – but that's half the fun. You'll be relieved to find the trig point surrounded by stone flags where you can comfortably sit for a brew while you prepare your next compass bearing. You've just bagged the first trig of the day!

> If visibility is poor, you may wish to turn back and retrace your steps at this point because in poor weather the centre of the plateau is a really easy place to get lost. The alternative is to take a shortcut across the moor back to Ringing Roger: from the trig pillar, a vague and boggy path heads south-west, crossing a couple of quintessential hags and groughs before picking up the path at the southern edge of the plateau. From here, you can turn left (east) back to Ringing Roger and descend to Edale using the outward route.

4 From the trig point, **walk on a bearing of 312°** (north-west) for 300m across the moor to meet the path along Blackden Edge. **Turn left** on to this path and follow it along the edge to the fords at Blackden Brook. After crossing the small fords of Blackden Brook, continue on the edge path to a gate (SK 115 884). Go through the gate and continue to work your way around the edge of the plateau, heading north for 400m and then veering west along Seal Edge. It's a fair way to the next trig point, so pause for snacks and enjoy the views from the many gritstone boulders that characterise the northern edge of the plateau. Keep going along the edge path all the way to the head of Fair Brook (SK 093 891). If visibility is good, this is a marvellous spot to perch on a rock for lunch and admire the view of Alport Moor and Bleaklow on the other side of the Snake Pass.

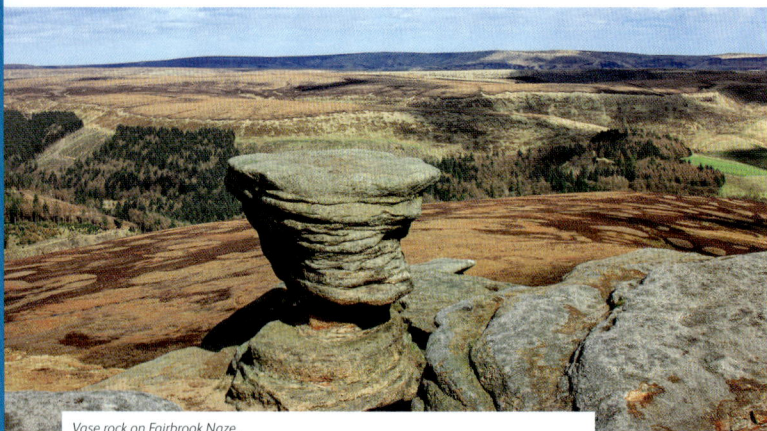
Vase rock on Fairbrook Naze.

5 **Turn sharp right** out of Fair Brook to follow a path that contours the edge of Kinder Scout in a Z-shape out to the spur of Fairbrook Naze. Head west from here, keeping to the high path along The Edge for 1.8km until you reach the third ford of Upper Red Brook (SK 079 897).

6 Cross the small ford (which may or may not have water flowing) and immediately **turn left** to follow a faint and narrow trod into the moor **on a bearing of 210°** for 400m to the next trig pillar – what a relief! This one stands at 624m and feels like it's in the middle of nowhere so enjoy the peace and quiet while it lasts. Keep your eyes peeled for a chance sighting of a mountain hare in this area, which may or may not be camouflaged depending on the season.

7 When you've had your fun getting up on to the trig pillar (and off again!), **walk on a bearing of 150°** for 100m to the corner of a fence, then follow the fence line for 150m down to the southern side of the plateau edge to join a footpath (if the fence has been moved or disappeared since the time of writing simply head south for about 200m from the trig pillar to locate the footpath).

8 **Turn left** on to the footpath (heading south-east along the plateau edge) and walk for 700m to reach the head of Kinder Downfall. Cross over the river at the head of Kinder Downfall (SK 083 889), which famously becomes an 'upfall' in very strong winds. **Turn sharp right** to continue along the edge path in a southerly direction (remember to look back towards the gorge to see the Downfall), picking your way between the rocks and making sure that you don't lose too much elevation.

The lonely trig point.

9 1km south of the Downfall, cross the ford at Red Brook (SK 080 879) and stay on the edge path for 600m. If in doubt, walk **on a bearing of 204°** until an obvious split of paths. **Take the left path** marked with a large cairn (SK 078 873), which initially trends gently uphill and then bends to the right at the boulders. It's about 400m to the trig pillar from the cairn. In good visibility, Kinder Low trig pillar will come into view between some large boulders. Walk towards this and take in the views of Pym Chair and the Pagoda to the east, or of Manchester and beyond to the west.

10 The paths and peat trods can be a bit confusing from the Kinder Low trig pillar, so it's best to **walk on a bearing of 104°** for 400m to Noe Stool – a giant anvil-shaped rock that sits close to the source of the River Noe at Edale Head. This short section is pathless and boggy but well trodden as a shortcut between the two points; just hold on to your walking boots!

11 **Heading east** from Noe Stool, the path drops down slightly and passes a large cairn before joining a flagstone path which gradually heads up towards a giant rock outcrop called the Pagoda – another excellent viewpoint and a great place to have a clamber about (the OS map only mentions Pym Chair, a smaller boulder behind the Pagoda). **Keep heading east** towards the Woolpacks – a sprawling cluster of weathered boulders named after their resemblance to the bales of wool carried by packhorses. There are pathless, boggy sections through the maze of boulders which can get confusing. It's worth walking **on a bearing of 75°** for 550m from the Pagoda to Crowden Tower to keep on track. Crowden Tower is a remarkable outcrop of boulders overlooking Crowden Brook.

Clare Kelly on the summit of The Edge trig pillar.

12 Pick up the path just behind Crowden Tower to drop down to the stream crossing at the head of Crowden Brook (SK 094 872). Enjoy the view here of Mam Tor framed by Crowden Brook's ravine. After crossing the shallow stream, cut up the steep bank to the **right** to rejoin the easterly path along the edge for about 750m.

13 **Turn right** at the junction (SK 103 871) to join a flagstone path that leads to the top of Grindslow Knoll. Where the flagstones end, walk up the steep grassy path to the top of the knoll. How far can you see from here? Take a final look before you start walking back down to Edale.

14 From the highest point on Grindslow Knoll, **walk about 50m on a bearing of 130°** to pick up the direct path to Edale. This heads steeply south-east for about 1km, eventually reaching a gate into open pasture. Take your time here as there are a lot of loose rocks. Walk down through the pasture until you reach a fingerpost marking the *Pennine Way*. **Turn left** to follow the path lined with trees back to Edale.

| GOOD TO KNOW

PUBLIC TRANSPORT AND ACCESS

Edale sits on the Manchester–Sheffield railway line and is well-served by trains daily.

There are pay & display car parks in Edale village and at the station; these can fill up early on fine weekends. The Edale Valley is situated just north of the Hope Valley and is easily accessible from the main A6187 road in Hope, or from Mam Nick on the Rushup Edge road west of Mam Tor.

WHEN TO WALK IT

This is a great outing all year round, but is particularly enjoyable in May when the moorland flora begins to show, and in summer when the bilberries are ripe and the heather creates a purple haze across the landscape.

It is best avoided in bad weather which can hang around on the plateau. The reduced (and at times zero) visibility and lack of landmarks can make it a frustrating and time-consuming task to navigate. As the plateau is a raised blanket bog it can be extremely challenging to walk on after heavy rainfall. Make sure you give yourself plenty of hours of daylight to complete this walk and carry a headtorch with spare batteries, especially during the shorter days of the year.

TERRAIN AND NAVIGATION

There are steep paths and rocky sections on the ascent, descent and along the edge, and the moorland section is exposed with faint paths/trods. There are short sections when a compass is required, but navigation is fairly straightforward as the route mostly follows the edges. It is advisable to carry a map and compass, and to know how to use them.

FACILITIES AND REFRESHMENTS

There are toilets at the car park and at the Edale visitor centre. The visitor centre also has a shop and can provide local information; it's next to the Fieldhead Campsite. The Penny Pot Cafe by Edale station is perfectly placed for pre- or post-walk refreshments. There's also a cafe at Newfold Farm further into the village, as well as a general store. There are a couple of pubs in the village – the Rambler Inn and the Old Nags Head.

DOGS AND KIDS

Livestock and ground-nesting birds mean Kinder is a dog-on-lead kind of place, particularly between 1 March and 31 July when it is the law under the CRoW Act that dogs must be on short leads.

If conditions look tricky (low visibility or sodden bog) when you get to the first trig point this walk is eminently escapable by taking a shortcut back across to Ringing Roger. It can be a good choice for fit and adventurous youngsters, but be warned: once you've committed to walking along the northern side of plateau from the top of Blackden Brook onwards, it's a long way back to Edale whichever way you go.

POINTS OF INTEREST

Kinder Scout is the highest point in the Peak District with a summit cairn at 636m on the moorland plateau.

Trig pillars were erected by Ordnance Survey during the retriangulation of Britain (1935–1962) to be used in the National Grid as accurate fixed points for mapping coordinates. Brigadier Martin Hotine was responsible for the design, planning and implementation of the retriangulation and he designed the iconic trig pillar.

/ APPENDIX

TOURIST INFORMATION

/ *www.visitpeakdistrict.com* – tourism information

/ *www.peakdistrict.gov.uk* – national park website, with tourism, conservation, travel and car park information

/ *www.nationaltrust.org.uk* – the National Trust manages Kinder Scout; search for 'Kinder and Edale' for helpful information

/ **Edale Visitor Centre,** by Fieldhead Campsite

SELECTED PUBS, CAFES & PLACES TO STAY

There are any number of good places to eat, drink and stay near Kinder. The following is just a selection. For more info, visit the websites listed above.

/ **The Old Nags Head**, Edale
www.the-old-nags-head.co.uk . . . . **T** 01433 670 291

/ **The Rambler Inn**, Edale
www.theramblerinn.co.uk . . . . **T** 01433 670 268

/ **Penny Pot Cafe**, Edale
www.pennypotcafe.com . . . . **T** 01433 670 688

/ **Newfold Farm**, Edale – camping, cafe and shop
www.newfoldfarmedale.com . . . . **T** 01433 670 401

/ **Fieldhead Campsite**, Edale
www.fieldheadcampsite.co.uk . . . . **T** 01433 670 386

/ **YHA Edale Activity Centre**
www.yha.org.uk/hostel/yha-edale-activity-centre . . . . **T** 0345 371 9514

/ **George Hotel**, Hayfield
www.georgehotelhayfield.org . . . . **T** 01663 745 295

/ **The Kinder Lodge**, Hayfield
www.kinder-lodge.co.uk . . . . **T** 01663 743 613

GEAR SHOPS

/ **Outside**, Hathersage
www.outside.co.uk

/ **Alpkit**, Hathersage
www.alpkit.com

/ **Go Outdoors**, Hathersage
www.gooutdoors.co.uk

Mermaid's Pool and Kinder Reservoir.

MOUNTAIN WEATHER

Both the Mountain Weather Information Service and Met Office provide dedicated mountain forecasts for the Peak District National Park.

| *www.mwis.org.uk*
| *www.metoffice.gov.uk* – forecast for summits and key places including Kinder Low

USEFUL WEBSITES

| *www.edale.org.uk* – lots of useful info about the village
| *www.adventuresmart.uk* – general planning and safety information
| *www.moorsforthefuture.org.uk* – restoring and protecting the uplands
| *www.kindertrespass.org.uk* – resources about 1932 Mass Kinder Trespass
| *heritagerecords.nationaltrust.org.uk* – discover more about the archaeology cared for by the National Trust
| *www.wildlifetrusts.org*

REFERENCES

| *The Book of Edale: Portrait of a High Peak Village*
The Edale Society, Halsgrove

| *The South Yorkshire Moors*
Christopher Goddard, Gritstone Publishing

| *Dark Peak Walks*
Paul Besley, Cicerone Press

| *Kinder Scout: The people's mountain*
Ed Douglas & John Beatty, Vertebrate Publishing

ABOUT THE AUTHOR

Sarah Lister is a qualified Hill and Moorland Leader based in Edale village at the foot of Kinder Scout. The landscape first captured her attention in 2016 and since then has inspired her work as a Career Coach and host of two podcasts, *Wild About Kinder* and *About The Adventure*. She finds Kinder Scout a curious place and invites you to explore its beautiful edges, moorland plateau, gritstone rocks, and hidden cloughs with her guiding hand.
www.abouttheadventure.com

© Sam Devito

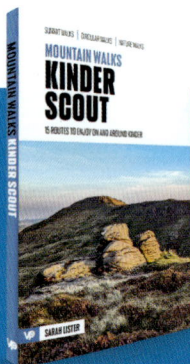

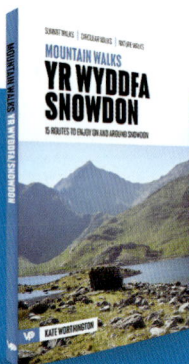

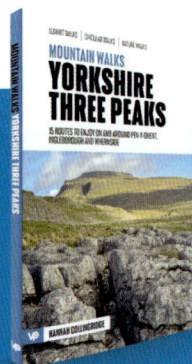